CityPack
Melbourne

ROD RITCHIE

Rod Ritchie, a freelance editor and travel writer, has been involved in Australian travel writing and publishing for nearly twenty years. He has written or contributed to numerous travel volumes and guidebooks. He is an inveterate traveller and keeps abreast of the latest travel data as the editor of various Australian travel maps and books.

City-centre map continues on inside back cover ◀

AA Publishing

Contents

About this book

CityPack Melbourne is divided into six sections to cover the six most important aspects of your visit to Melbourne. It includes:

- The city and its people
- Itineraries, walks and excursions
- The top 25 sights to visit
- What makes the city special
- Restaurants, hotels, shops and nightlife
- Practical information

In addition, easy-to-read side panels provide extra facts and snippets, highlights of places to visit and practical advice.

CROSS-REFERENCES

To help you make the most of your visit, cross-references, indicated by ▶, show you where to find additional information about a place or subject.

MAPS

The fold-out map in the wallet at the back of the book is a comprehensive street plan of Melbourne. All the map references given in the book refer to this map. For example, the State Parliament House in Spring Street has the following information: ✚ 21R indicating the grid square of the map in which the State Parliament House will be found. The Greater Melbourne map, referred to as the GM map, can be found alongside the Central Melbourne (fold-out) map.
The city-centre maps found on the inside front and back covers of the book itself are for quick reference. They show the top 25 sights, described on pages 24–48, which are clearly plotted by number (**1** – **25**), not by page number.

ADMISSION CHARGES

An indication of the admission charge for all attractions is given by categorising the standard adult rate as follows: ✋ expensive (over A$10), ✋ moderate (A$5–A$10) and ✋ inexpensive (under A$5).

MELBOURNE
life

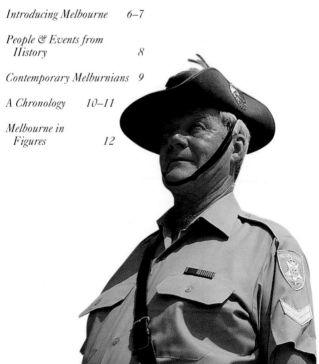

INTRODUCING MELBOURNE

Sophisticated, prosperous and European, vibrant and well-planned, Melbourne exudes order and certainty. Set astride the quiet waters of the Yarra River, it was founded in the mid-19th century and expanded rapidly after the discovery of gold nearby in 1851. Some of the world's finest Victorian architecture is here, alongside tall glass and steel office towers. Yet the old blends surprisingly well with the new, and today's modern, cosmopolitan metropolis with its tree-lined boulevards, its new public buildings, its efficient public transport and its profusion of parks and gardens, is one of Australia's most livable cities.

Dressing up for the Melbourne Cup

The Melbourne Cup

On the first Tuesday of November, Australia comes to a halt to watch the nation's richest and most prestigious horse race, the Melbourne Cup. Run over 2 miles, this handicap race carries prize money of over 2 million Australian dollars. At this notoriously unpredictable race, everyone becomes a gambler as they try to pick the winner. For Melburnians, race day is a public holiday and many make their way to the racetrack at Flemington to view the spectacle and have a good time.

Melbourne is the country's second largest community after Sydney, with 3.3 million inhabitants representing over 70 cultures. The cultural variety of the more recent arrivals has melded well with the predominantly Anglo-Saxon population to produce a vigorous society living in relative harmony. Most new arrivals tend to leave the past behind and settle down to enjoy a peaceful life. Is the social cohesion among much of the city's population due to the popularity of Australian Rules Football? Some say yes. This sport, unique to Australia, is followed with religious fervour.

Melburnians are generally as passionate about the arts as they are about sport. Here cabaret, comedy and all kinds of music thrive side-by-side with high culture. A major centre for the arts and the administrative centre of many Australian cultural institutions, Melbourne has also been the location for many of Australia's film productions, such as local director Paul Cox's *Innocence* (2000). The collection of the National Gallery of Victoria is world-class, displaying both international and Australian art including a unique Aboriginal collection.

This is also a city for food-lovers, with over 4,000 cafés and restaurants, and dining alfresco is a local passion. Many of Australia's wines are produced in the region. Melbourne is also the most fashion-conscious of all Australia's state capital cities.

To get the full picture of Melbourne, head for the suburbs. Carlton, northeast of the city centre, has an Italian population and Fitzroy is slightly bohemian. Richmond, to the east, has a flourishing Greek and Vietnamese subculture, while South Yarra is trendy. Further south is St Kilda, with its good restaurants and its beach.

Melbourne is also the capital of the state of Victoria, the smallest of the mainland states, and attractions are very accessible, both in and out of town. Only an hour's drive from the city you can see Australia's unique and often shy wildlife: the koala, kangaroo, wombat, platypus, emu, lyrebird and fairy penguin. These unique creatures are the inhabitants of an island continent that is part of one of the oldest land masses on earth.

So take your time, go with the flow, relax and enjoy this friendly city.

An aerial view of the city showing the Hoddle and Morrell bridges, spanning the Yarra River

Getting around

The metropolitan region is vast (around 72km north–south and 50km east–west). Melbourne's well planned Central Business District (CBD) consists of wide streets in a grid pattern. Since there is often some distance between the important sights, acquaint yourself with the city's excellent trams, which provide a first-rate service, including a free circle route around the CBD. An efficient and comprehensive rail and bus network covers the rest of the city.

7

PEOPLE & EVENTS FROM HISTORY

Aboriginal presence

The Aboriginal people of the Port Phillip area lived in harmony with nature and by their traditional means for thousands of years before European settlement. The nearly 40 different tribal groups throughout present-day Victoria were descendants of people who made their way to the Australian mainland from Southeast Asia up to 50,000 years ago, and led a semi-nomadic existence. Hunting and gathering for sustenance, the people were bonded to their surroundings by a complex system of spiritual beliefs and their lives were governed by cultural codes handed down through the generations.

The dangers of the gold-rush days

BATMAN & HIS DEAL

John Batman effectively dispossessed the Aboriginal people living in the Melbourne area in 1835 when he traded blankets, axes and the like for 593,040 acres of tribal lands, although this deal held no legal validity. By 1840, the year of Batman's death, white settlement was unstoppable, and the new town had a population of 10,000.

PASTORAL EXPANSION & GOLD FEVER

From the 1840s the fertile interior of Victoria was explored and opened for pastoral settlement. Grazing and agriculture became the economic basis for the towns that sprang up to support these rural pursuits, and Melbourne was proclaimed a city in 1847. With the discovery of gold near Ballarat in 1851, the state really forged ahead. Prospectors flocked to Victoria from all over the world and the population quadrupled within a decade.

BOOM & BUST

From the time of the gold rush onwards, and culminating in the Great Exhibition of 1888, the city of Melbourne enjoyed boom times created by the state's enormous mineral wealth. However, the bubble burst in the 1890s and the period of great economic depression that followed ruined numerous speculators and brought great hardship to many.

Contemporary Melburnians

GERMAINE GREER

Arguably Australia's greatest cultural export, Germaine Greer, born in 1939, is a writer, academic, broadcaster and publisher who lectures at Cambridge University. The feminist classic *The Female Eunuch* brought her fame in 1969, and she is the author of a string of other best-selling works, including the acclaimed *The Whole Woman* (1999).

MICHAEL LEUNIG

The whimsical images of this cartoonist, born in 1945, first appeared in *Newsday* and *London Oz* and are now a regular feature in the daily newspapers *The Age* and the *Sydney Morning Herald*. Michael Leunig's challenging and in-sightful cartoons have been published in over ten books, and his works can be seen on gallery walls as well as on trams and buses.

KYLIE MINOGUE

One of Australia's most successful pop singing sensations, Kylie Minogue, born in 1968, started her career as Charlene in the long-running televison series *Neighbours*. Her late 1980s hits 'Locomotion' and 'I Should Be So Lucky' topped the charts, and she appeared in films such as *The Delinquents* and *Streetfighter*. She has since been back in the charts again.

SIR IAN POTTER

A visionary businessman, stockbroker and company director, Sir Ian Potter (1902–94) was the founder and benefactor of the Ian Potter Foundation, a charitable trust that supports a broad range of activities in the field of the arts, including ballet and opera, as well as the environment, education and health.

ARCHIE ROACH

Aboriginal singer and songwriter Archie Roach, born in 1955, made a name for himself through his albums 'Charcoal Lane' and 'Jamu Dream-ing.' He has received numerous awards including a Mo Award, presented by the music industry for excellence in live performance.

Famous Melburnians

Before Australia got into its cultural stride in the 1970s, it was hard for talented writers, actors and performers to make it big here. Consequently, Melburnians such as comedian Barry Humphries, feminist writer Germaine Greer and the singer Nick Cave had to go overseas to further their careers.

The new order

There are probably more vestiges of the old class system based on wealth and social position in Melbourne, especially among those of British descent, than in other Australian capital cities. A new order emerged, however, as hard-working immigrant families, most of whom arrived after World War II, prospered in the 1950s and 60s. Since then, many Asian immigrants, particularly from Vietnam, have set up family businesses and followed the same path to prosperity.

A CHRONOLOGY

40,000–60,000 years ago	Aboriginal people arrive from Southeast Asia.
1770	Captain James Cook and the crew of the *Endeavour* arrive in Botany Bay, near the present location of Sydney.
1779	Suggestions are made in England that New South Wales could become a penal colony.
1787	The First Fleet departs from Portsmouth, England. The 11 ships carry 1,400 people, comprising 756 convicts and a contingent of 644 soldiers.
1788	The First Fleet arrives in Botany Bay on 20 January. The commander and first governor of the colony, Captain Arthur Phillip, moves north to Port Jackson (Sydney Harbour). The colony of New South Wales is proclaimed.
1793	The first free settlers land in Sydney.
1803	The British send ships to Port Phillip Bay to prevent French settlement.
1804	Australia's second major settlement is founded at Hobart, Tasmania.
1817	Governor Macquarie first refers to the colony as 'Australia' in official correspondence.
1832	During the next 20 years over 200,000 people emigrate to Australia, mostly from Britain, under the government's assisted emigration programme.
1835	John Batman buys land around Port Phillip Bay from the Aboriginal people. Two years later, the site is renamed Melbourne, after the British Prime Minister.
1851	Gold is discovered near Ballarat. People flock to the area from all over the world and Melbourne's population multiplies rapidly. The colony of Victoria separates from New South Wales.

1860s	As Melbourne prospers, the foundations are laid for many grand buildings.
1861	The first Melbourne Cup is run.
1883	The first railway service begins between Melbourne and Sydney.
1890s	Economic depression ends boom times.
1901	The Commonwealth of Australia is proclaimed, joining the six Australian colonies into a federation; the first Commonwealth Parliament opens in Melbourne.
1918	World War I ends. Sixty thousand Australians have died.
1927	Federal Parliament opens in Canberra.
1929	The Great Depression begins.
1934	Australia's national airline, Qantas, begins regular flights from Sydney to London.
1939	Black Friday bush fires kill 71 people in Victoria.
1939–45	Australian troops fight overseas during World War II, with over 35,000 war deaths.
1947	Post-war immigration from Europe brings much-needed skilled labour for industry.
1956	First television broadcast in Melbourne. The city hosts the XVI Olympiad.
1972	Australia's involvement in Vietnam ends, with 496 servicemen killed.
1994	Native Title Bill becomes law.
1999	Australia votes against becoming a Republic.
2001	The Australian nation celebrates a centenary of Federation.

11

MELBOURNE IN FIGURES

Geography
- Latitude 37° 176 49' south, longitude 144 ° 176 58' east on the southeast edge of Australia.
- At 37° 176 49' south, Melbourne lies at a similar latitude to New York, San Francisco, Cape Town, Beijing, Istanbul and Lisbon.
- Melbourne is 16,599km from New York, 13,258km from San Francisco, 17,450km from London (via Singapore) and 8,143km from Tokyo.
- Slightly smaller than the United Kingdom, the state of Victoria covers an area of 277,560 sq km.
- Victoria's southernmost point, Wilsons Promontory, is the southernmost point of mainland Australia.

People
- From the 10,000 people who lived in Melbourne in 1840, the city's population has grown to over 3.3 million.
- More than 70 different nationalities make up Melbourne's population.
- During the gold rushes of the 1850s, Melbourne trebled its size in only three years and, until the 1890s, was Australia's largest city. About 40,000 Chinese immigrants came to the goldfields in the 1850s.
- Just over 10,000 people of Aboriginal descent live in Melbourne.
- Post World War II migration was predominately from European countries; since the mid-1970s most immigrants have come from Southeast Asia.

City Statistics
- Greater Melbourne covers 1,700sq km, compared with New York's 1,523sq km London's 1,560sq km and Sydney's 4,248sq km.
- Melbourne sprawls 50km from east to west.
- Area of the City of Melbourne – 36sq km.
- Area of the Central Buisness District (CBD) – 2.6sq km.
- Total area of parkland in the city – 563ha.
- Total length of roads in the city – 315km.
- Tallest structure – the Rialto Tower, completed in1986, at 253m.
- Oldest building – the Mitre Tavern, 5–9 Bank Place, built in 1837.

MELBOURNE
how to organise your time

13

ITINERARIES

There are regular tram services in Melbourne's centre and 18 of the Top 25 sights are within a 20-minute walk of most Central Business District hotels.

ITINERARY ONE	**THE CENTRAL BUSINESS DISTRICT**
Morning	Start at the ANZ Gothic Bank (➤ 54) for a look at its magnificent interior. Walk for two blocks along Collins Street towards King Street and take the high-speed lift to the observation deck of Rialto Towers (➤ 34). Continue down King Street and cross Flinders Street to the Melbourne Aquarium (➤ 40).
Lunch	Have lunch in the café at the aquarium.
Afternoon	Walk back to Flinders Street, turn right and walk to the Immigration Museum (➤ 42), where you can research family history and view immigration memorabilia. Take a tram along Flinders Street, past Flinders Street Station (➤ 60) to the Gold Treasury Museum (➤ 52) and Parliament House (➤ 55).
ITINERARY TWO	**NORTH OF THE CBD**
Morning	Trams are the best transport to the following attractions. Start the day at the Queen Victoria Market (➤ 27). Take a tram east along Victoria Street to the Melbourne Museum (➤ 25).
Lunch	Have lunch at the Museum café or picnic in Carlton Gardens with some produce from the morning market.
Afternoon and evening	Walk to nearby Old Melbourne Gaol (➤ 30) or to Brunswick Street, Fitzroy (➤ 32) and spend the evening dining and window shopping.
ITINERARY THREE	**SOUTHBANK & THE ARTS CENTRE**
Morning	Visit the Victorian Arts Centre (➤ 36), then walk along St Kilda Road to the National Gallery of Victoria (➤ 41).

Southbank and the Southgate complex

Lunch

Have lunch at the Blue Train Café (► 68) or The Deck (► 68) in the nearby Southgate complex at Southbank.

Afternoon

Relax on a Yarra River cruise (► 29), then spend the rest of the afternoon at the Crown Entertainment Complex (► 28).

ITINERARY FOUR   **PARKS & GARDENS**

Morning

Walk through Treasury Gardens, then through Fitzroy Gardens (► 39) and visit historic Cook's Cottage.
Cross Wellington Street and walk along Jolimont Street to the Australian Gallery of Sport and the Melbourne Cricket Ground (► 31).

Lunch

Have lunch at Sonic (► 63) near the MCG or continue on to the Observatory Gate Café in the Royal Botanic Gardens (► 24).

Afternoon

Cross the Swan Street Bridge to Kings Domain (► 37), view Government House (► 54) and the first governor's cottage (► 37), visit the Shrine of Remembrance (► 37) and explore the Royal Botanic Gardens (► 24).

15

WALKS

INFORMATION

Distance 8km
Time 2 hours one way on foot or
40 minutes on a bike
Start point St Kilda Pier
✚ 7L
End point Green Point
✚ see Greater Melbourne (GM)
map
▣ Tram 16 from Swanston
Street

The popular St Kilda Pier

ST KILDA BAY TRAIL

Although regarded as Melbourne's liveliest suburb, St Kilda (➤ 47) also has a peaceful aspect—a lovely bay with walkways, parks and skyline views. There are numerous stopping-off points for coffee breaks and plenty of opportunities at the start of your walk to diverge into busy Acland Street for a snack.

From St Kilda Pier (where you can rent bicycles and roller blades) this walk follows the bay all the way south to Green Point at Brighton Beach. Side tracks lead to local streets. Depending on the day of the week and the weather, there is likely to be activity around the water, from families wading to wind surfers going full tilt before the wind, jumping the waves as they fly. All types of yachts can often be seen out on the bay, and many more are moored at marinas along the trail.

At Point Ormond, a vantage point affords fine views of both sides of the bay. A further 3km, next to Middle Brighton Pier, is Melbourne's only remaining saltwater swimming pool. Nearby, at Dendy Street, are the colorful bathing boxes, remnants from the early-19th century still used by bathers for changing. Less than a kilometre remains to the end of this walk, Green Point. You could retrace your steps to return to St Kilda, or take a taxi back.

CITY HERITAGE WALK

To learn about Melbourne's past and how the city developed, take the excellent, self-guided 'Melbourne's Golden Mile' walk through the city's historical area, streets, arcades and lanes. Along the way be sure to visit the magnificent old buildings and museums for the total heritage experience.

Begin at the Immigration Museum, then head for King Street, via William Street and Flinders Lane. Watch for the old bluestone buildings along here, before turning into Collins Street. Just next to the Rialto Towers, check out the old Rialto Hotel and the nearby ornate office buildings dating from the late 19th century. Taking a detour along William Street to Little Collins and back to Collins via Bank Place, you will pass the grand old Australia Club (William Street), the impressive Stalbridge Chambers (Little Collins Street), and the Mitre Tavern (Bank Place).

Back in Collins Street, view the ornate banking chamber of the ANZ Gothic Bank, the adjacent Banking Museum and the Cathedral Room of the former stock exchange. Just past Elizabeth Street, look for the entrance to the Block Arcade and follow this covered shopping area through to the Royal Arcade in Little Collins Street. Return to Little Collins Street and turn into Howey Place; walk to Capitol Arcade, past the art deco Capitol Theatre, into Swanston Street, and back into Collins Street.

After inspecting the grand old Melbourne Town Hall, proceed down Collins Street towards Spring Street to see its three blocks of fine churches, theatres, shops and the exclusive Melbourne Club. In Spring Street, visit the historic Gold Treasury, the splendid Windsor Hotel, the State Parliament House and the majestic Princess Theatre. To reach Carlton Gardens and the Melbourne Museum, take a detour down Little Bourke Street, with its colourful Chinatown, and then follow Punch Lane, Lonsdale Street and Exhibition Street.

THE SIGHTS

- Immigration Museum (➤ 42)
- Rialto Towers (➤ 34)
- Melbourne Town Hall
- Arcades
- Gold Treasury Museum (➤ 52)
- State Parliament House (➤ 55)
- Chinatown (➤ 43)
- Melbourne Museum (➤ 25)

INFORMATION

Distance 4km
Time 2hrs 30 mins–3hrs 30 mins
Start point Immigration Museum
✚ 19T
End point Melbourne Museum
✚ 21P; 7G
ℹ Brochure: ☎ 9654 2288

Interior of the ANZ Gothic Bank, Collins Street

EVENING STROLLS

INFORMATION

Melbourne Town Hall to Southbank
Distance 1km
Time 30–60 minutes
Start point Melbourne Town Hall
➕ 20S
End point Southbank
➕ 20T; 7H

Gothic Bank to Parliament House
Distance 1km
Time 1–2 hours
Start point ANZ Gothic Bank, 386 Collins Street
➕ 19S
End point State Parliament House
➕ 21

Caution

These streets are well frequented at most times, but it's best to walk with a companion in the evening.

Southbank Promenade

MELBOURNE TOWN HALL TO SOUTHBANK

This pleasant walk down one of the city's main streets leads past the famous Young and Jackson's Hotel to Flinders Street Station (➤ 60). Just opposite is the new Federation Square. Cross the Yarra River over the historic Princes Bridge with its great views. Take the Southbank Promenade to the west of the bridge and stroll past the shopping complex to the Crown Entertainment Complex (➤ 28).

ANZ GOTHIC BANK TO PARLIAMENT HOUSE

Most of this walk is eastward along Collins Street past some of Melbourne's best addresses. On Friday nights shops remain open until 9PM, at other times they ususally close at 6PM. Start at the ANZ Gothic Bank (➤ 54) and walk east, passing Australia on Collins and Collins 234 shopping centres. Continue until you come to the Town Hall. Its City Experience Centre provides information on Melbourne. Take a break in City Square for a coffee at the café, before viewing the nearby ornate Regent Theatre (➤ 78). This part of Collins Street, just past the Russell Street intersection, is pretty at night with its strings of white lights. The Gold Treasury Museum (➤ 52) is opposite where Collins Street ends. Turn left and walk up Spring Street, past the Windsor Hotel , to the State Parliament House (➤ 55).

ORGANISED SIGHTSEEING

The city skyline

AAT KINGS TOURS

This experienced operator specialises in bus tours of the city sights, Mt Buller, the Great Ocean Road, Phillip Island, Sovereign Hill and other major destinations. ☎ 9274 7422

AUSTRALIAN PACIFIC TOURS

Guided bus tours take in the Great Ocean Road, the Dandenong Ranges and Phillip Island. There's also a special Mt Buller Snow Tour from June to October. ☎ 9663 1611

CITY CIRCLE TRAM

This free tram starts at 10AM daily and runs at 10-minute intervals around the CBD perimeter to many of the main sights until 6PM. ☎ 131 638

CITY EXPLORER

Perfect for a one-hour or all-day trip, this hop-on, hop-off service offers 18 stops and discount entrance fees for the attractions it passes. ☎ 9650 7000

GRAY LINE

This international company offers an extensive selection of day tours to a range of destinations, including the Grampians, the Snowfields, the city, the Dandenong Ranges and Yarra Valley. ☎ 9663 4455

VICTORIAN HARLEY RIDES

Trips to city and scenic sights, the Great Ocean Road and the Dandenong Ranges, all aboard a chauffeured Harley Davidson. ☎ 9761 1647

Walking tours

Melbourne's flat terrain makes walking very easy. If you are interested in Melbourne's historic area and architecture, joining a guided walking tour is an excellent option. Guided tours include: Melbourne Book Lovers' Walk (☎ 0412 012 904); Aboriginal Heritage Walks (☎ 9252 2300); City Pub Walks (☎ 9384 0655); Walk About Melbourne Tours (☎ 9562 0034); Melbourne Heritage Walks (☎ 9827 1085); and Foodies Dream Tours (☎ 9320 5822).

Victoria Winery Tours

Small groups travel to the vineyards of the Yarra Valley, Macedon Ranges and Mornington Peninsula with a flexible itinerary. Other tours include the Thoroughbred Tour, the Two-Day Romantic Escape and the Melbourne Wholesale Market Experience (☎ 9621 2089).

Excursions

INFORMATION

Geelong and the Bellarine Peninsula

Distance Around 72km from Melbourne to Geelong and an extra 31km to Queenscliff

Time Allow a full day

🚌 Bus tour available

⛴ Ferry from Queenscliff to Sorrento (☎ 5258 3244)

ℹ️ Geelong Visitor Information Centre (☎ 1800 620 888). National Wool Museum (☎ 5227 0701)

Mornington Peninsula

Distance 97km from Melbourne to Portsea

Time Allow a full day

Victoria Winery Tours

☎ 9621 1413

ℹ️ Peninsula Visitor Centre (☎ 5987 3078)

Point Lonsdale on the Bellarine Peninsula

GEELONG & THE BELLARINE PENINSULA

Geelong, Victoria's second largest city, is only an hour's drive from Melbourne. The city waterfront at Corio Bay, the gateway to the Bellarine Peninsula, is full of restored old buildings dating from the 1880s to the 1920s, waterfront boulevards, and dozens of fine cafés and restaurants. The National Wool Museum (➤ 72) is in an old bluestone warehouse. Nearby Queenscliff, one of Victoria's most popular winter and weekend escapes, has many fine Victorian stone buildings, including Fort Queenscliff and the Maritime Museum, which explores local nautical history.

MORNINGTON PENINSULA

Running southeast from Melbourne around Port Phillip Bay, the Nepean Highway allows access to sparkling bays, beaches, waterfront promenades and magnificent coastal scenery. The low-key bayside towns of Mt Eliza, Mornington, Dromana, Rosebud, Rye, Sorrento and Portsea offer quiet beaches, golf courses, hedge mazes (➤ 56) and wineries as well as good food and accommodation. On the Western Port side of the peninsula lie the rugged surfing beaches and the seaside suburbs of Hastings and Flinders. Stony Point is the stepping-off point to nearby French Island (➤ 50), where you can see colonies of koalas.

GREAT OCEAN ROAD

One of the world's great coastal drives, the spectacular journey from Torquay, southwest of Melbourne, to Warrnambool and beyond encompasses rainforests, seaside beach towns, cliffs, mountain eucalypt forests and dramatic offshore rock formations. Past Torquay, the surfing capital of Australia, is the popular seaside town of Lorne; nearby Apollo Bay is a fishing port. Port Campbell National Park is home to the amazing Twelve Apostles, natural rock formations, standing like sentinels above the ocean. Loch Ard Gorge, the site of a legendary shipwreck, is also worth seeing. Warrnambool is the regional capital, while antique Portland is Victoria's oldest town.

YARRA VALLEY

Northeast of Melbourne, the Yarra River is very different than it is in the city. In the pretty town of Eltham, don't miss the artists' colony at Montsalvat (► 52). At Yering, the Yarra Valley Dairy (► 69) offers handmade cheeses and local cuisine. At the turn of the 20th century, 75 percent of all Australian wines came from Victoria, and the Yarra Valley was one of the most productive wine regions in Australia. Today nearly 20 percent of the nation's wines are produced in this region and its 35 vineyards welcome visitors and sell on their premises. Further on is Healesville Sanctuary (► 56), with its native animal species in natural surroundings of bushland and wetlands, and the nearby Galeena Beek Living Cultural Centre, where you can learn about Aboriginal culture and art. Many bus tours run to this district.

The Twelve Apostles

INFORMATION

Great Ocean Road
Distance 349km to Warrnamboool from Melbourne
Time Allow a full day
🛈 Geelong & Great Ocean Road Visitor Centre (☎ 5275 5797)
AAT Kings Tours
☎ 9274 7422
Gray Line Tours
☎ 9663 4455
Australian PacifiicTours
☎ 1300 655 965

Yarra Valley
Distance 26km to Montsalvat
Time Allow a full day
Australian Pacific Tour
☎ 9663 1611
Galeena Beek
✉ Glen Eadie Avenue, Healesville
☎ 5962 1119
Montsalvat
✉ Hillcrest Avenue, Eltham
☎ 9439 7712
Yarra Valley Dairy
✉ McMeikans Road, Yering
☎ 9739 0023
Victoria Winery Tours
☎ 9621 1413
🛈 Yarra Valley Visitor Information Centre (☎ 5962 2600)

WHAT'S ON

The best way to find out what's on in and around Melbourne is to check the entertainment pages of *The Age* every Friday. Its 24-page entertainment guide, *EG*, has details on everything from opera to free outdoor events. Other useful publications are giveaways such as *This Week in Melbourne* and *The Official Visitors' Guide*, found at hotels, tourist information booths and attractions. Major events include:

January   *Cricket matches*: They take place day and night at the famous Melbourne Cricket Ground.
Australian Open Tennis: The classic tournament is at Melbourne Park.

March   *Qantas Australian Grand Prix*: Albert Park.
The Moomba Festival: A Melbourne cultural institution that includes parades and exhibitions.

April   *Melbourne Food and Wine Festival*: The place to sample Australia's best food and wines.
Melbourne International Flower and Garden Show: Indoor exhibition of plants and garden products.
Melbourne International Comedy Festival: One of the largest comedy festivals in the world.
Rip Curl Pro and Sun Smart Classic: Australia's most prestigious surfing event is held at Torquay.

June   *Melbourne International Film Festival*: A showcase for top local and international movies.

August   *Australian Antiques and Fine Art Fair*: The state's premier antiques fair.

September   *Australian Rules Grand Final*: The city comes to a halt as the top teams compete.
Royal Melbourne Show: Eleven days of animals, events, food, art, crafts and more.

October/November   *Melbourne Cup and the Spring Racing Carnival*: The Melbourne Cup is the highlight of this series of prestigious races.
Melbourne Festival: Art exhibitions, concerts, plays and dance performances.

December   *New Year's Eve*: Fireworks and partying all over the city.

MELBOURNE's
top 25 sights

The sights are shown on the maps on the inside front cover and
inside back cover, numbered **1–25**

ROYAL BOTANIC GARDENS

INFORMATION

- 22V; 8H
- Birdwood Avenue
- Recorded message
  9252 2364.
  Aboriginal Heritage Walks
  9252 2300
- Gardens: Apr–Oct: daily
  7:30AM–8:30PM. Nov–Mar:
  daily 7:30AM–5:30PM.
  Aboriginal Heritage Walks
  Thu, Sun 11AM
- Observatory Café
- Tram 8 to Stop 21
- Excellent
- Free
- Melbourne City Centre
  (➤ 26), Southbank and
  the Crown Complex (➤ 28),
  Yarra River (➤ 29),
  Melbourne Cricket Ground
  (➤ 31), Victorian Arts
  Centre (➤ 36), Kings
  Domain (➤ 37), Fitzroy
  Gardens (➤ 39), National
  Gallery of Victoria (➤ 41)
- Guided tours available

One of the world's finest botanic gardens, this is a pleasant place to be on a hot summer's day, when you feel like some early morning exercise or a break from the city's bustle. Check out the free guided tours and open-air performances.

The gardens Established in 1846 by the famous botanist Baron von Meuller, these world-acclaimed gardens covering about 36ha were superbly landscaped by William Guilfoyle, who created them in the 18th-century English tradition with rolling lawns, formal flower gardens and wooded coppices. Today more than 12,000 plant species from around the world are in all stages of bud and blossom at any given time. From June to August the camellias are at their best. In spring, between September and November, roses, azaleas and rhododendrons bloom. On a summer's day, Fern Gully is a cool, tranquil spot, with a resident colony of flying foxes resting in the trees. Don't miss the Australian rainforest section, where many species are identified, along with information about the particular location in Australia that they come from.

Observatory Gate This entrance to the gardens is the ideal orientation point for your visit. At the visitor centre you can book a guided tour, browse the gardens, shop for unusual gifts and souvenirs, and enjoy a meal or snack in the excellent Observatory Café.

Aboriginal Heritage Walks On these, guides share their knowledge of the area and the life of the Bunurong and Woiwurrung people, occupiers of the Melbourne area before Europeans arrived. You'll learn about their culture and use of indigenous plants.

MELBOURNE MUSEUM

This ultra-modern museum devoted to the art, culture and nature of Melbourne and the surrounding area, uses interaction, performance and technology. It stands in Carlton Gardens, opposite the grand 19th-century Royal Exhibition Building.

Museum exhibitions Major touring exhibitions supplement the collections of this museum. The Bunjilaka Aboriginal Centre tells the stories of Victorian Aborigines, and explores their complex relationship with the land and issues relating to Aboriginal laws, property and knowledge. The People and Places Gallery focuses primarily on Melbourne's history and presents historical stories, artefacts, images and soundscapes to introduce Australian society. In the impressive Forest Gallery you walk among living trees, plants, animals, birds and insects; five interpretive zones explain the effects of fire, water, earth movement, climate and humans on the forests around Melbourne. Exhibitions in the Science Gallery show how much science shapes our world. Technology exhibitions explore the rapid evolution of digital technology and its effects on our daily lives. Check out the intricate workings of human beings in the noted Mind and Body Gallery. Nearby at the Children's Museum, in a huge, colourful, cube-shaped building, kids and their families are encouraged to engage with interactive exhibitions. The popular IMAX cinema is in the complex, along with shops and cafés.

HIGHLIGHTS

- Bunjilaka Aboriginal Centre
- Decorative Arts section
- Children's Discovery Centre
- IMAX cinema
- Forest Gallery
- Science Gallery

INFORMATION

- ⊞ 21P; 7G
- ✉ Melbourne Museum, Carlton Gardens, Carlton
- ☎ 9651 6777
- ✉ IMAX Theatre, Rathdowne Street, Carlton
- ☎ 9663 5454
- 🕐 Daily 9–6
- 🍴 Café and restaurant
- 🚃 City Circle Tram
- ♿ Excellent
- 💰 Moderate
- ↔ Melbourne City Centre (► 26), Queen Victoria Market (► 27),
- ❓ Guided tours

Phar Lap, Australia's most famous racehorse

3

MELBOURNE CITY CENTRE

HIGHLIGHTS

- Lanes and arcades
- Department stores
- Old arcades
- Specialist shops
- Historic buildings

INFORMATION

- 20S; 7G
- Victoria Visitor Information Centre, corner of Swanston and Little Collins streets; City Experience Centre, Melbourne Town Hall, Swanston Street
- Victoria Tourism Information Service: 132 842
- Mon–Fri 9–6; Sat, Sun and public hols 9–4
- Many cafés and restaurants
- City Circle Tram
- Varies
- Royal Botanic Gardens (▶ 24), Queen Victoria Market (▶ 27), Southbank and the Crown Complex (▶ 28), Yarra River (▶ 29), Melbourne Trams (▶ 33), Rialto Towers Observation Deck (▶ 34), Immigration Museum (▶ 42), Chinatown (▶ 43)
- Shopping hours may vary, but city shops are generally open Mon–Thu 10–6; Fri, 10–9; Sat, Sun 10–5

Compact and easy to explore, the centre of Melbourne is set out in a rectangular grid. When you get tired of walking, just jump on a tram – the one that operates around the perimeter of the Central Business District is free.

City centre Most of the main department stores, hotels, offices and banks, as well as the fine old Victorian churches, theatres and public institutions that give Melbourne its personality are found here. Excellent restaurants and cafés are scattered throughout the city centre. Within walking distance, across the Yarra River to the south, are parks and gardens, the Victorian Arts Centre and National Gallery of Victoria, the Southgate shopping and dining complex on Southbank, and the Crown Casino. The best way to get a sense of the place is on foot, with occasional rides on the free City Circle Tram.

Shopping Melbourne has great shopping opportunities. The retail area is bounded roughly by Elizabeth, Collins, Spring and La Trobe streets. Check out the city's lanes and arcades, especially the Royal and Block Arcades. Look for Hardware Lane, a stretch of old warehouses between Bourke and Lonsdale streets, converted into restaurants, bars and shops.

Hardware Street at lunchtime

4

QUEEN VICTORIA MARKET

Some of the original buildings still stand at Australia's biggest and most popular outdoor market, which offers just about everything from food, footwear and clothing to plants, art and souvenirs. There has been a market on the site since 1859.

History Just a few minutes' walk from the city centre, this bustling, chaotic retail complex is the city's largest market with over a thousand stalls on 7ha. The complex is the last of several city markets, which have disappeared since the construction of large shopping centres in the suburbs. Many of the present buildings date back to the 19th century, including the Meat Hall (1869), Sheds A to F (1878), and the two-storey shops on Victoria Street (1887).

Markets The colourful traders are an attraction in their own right, promoting their wares and bantering with passersby. In the Lower Market are the Meat Hall, with meat, fish and game; the Dairy Hall, featuring delicatessens, bakeries, patisseries and confectioneries; and a section with fresh fruit and vegetables, as well as a huge range of ready-to-eat foods, to take home or to devour as you stroll about the premises. Situated on a nearby rise, a stretch of open-sided sheds, known as the Upper Market, house an enormous variety of fresh produce, clothing, souvenirs, plants and everyday items for sale. On Sundays, a wine market operates here.

Guided tours The Foodies Dream Tour (➤ 19) provides a chance to taste Australian cheeses, nuts, preserves, meats and exotic tropical fruits, while the Heritage Market Tour (➤ 19) takes you through the market's original buildings and describes a century of its fascinating past.

HIGHLIGHTS

- The stallholders
- Stalls selling exotic tropical fruits and Australian cheeses
- Historic buildings
- Market tours
- Sunday Wine Market

INFORMATION

- 18Q; 6G
- Corner of Elizabeth and Victoria streets
- Information: 9320 5822. Tours: 9320 5835
- Tue, Thu 6–2; Fri 6–6; Sat 6–3; Sun 9–4
- Many cafés and restaurants nearby and plenty of stalls selling snack food and coffee
- Melbourne Central
- Any tram in Elizabeth northbound to stop 12
- Moderate
- Melbourne City Centre (➤ 26), Yarra River (➤ 29), Melbourne Trams (➤ 33), Rialto Towers Observation Deck (➤ 34), Immigration Museum (➤ 42), Chinatown (➤ 43)

SOUTHBANK & THE CROWN COMPLEX

HIGHLIGHTS

- River promenade
- Public art
- Shopping
- Cinemas
- Nightclubs
- Casino

INFORMATION

- ✚ 20T; 7H
- ✉ Crown Entertainment Complex, Southbank
- ☎ 9292 8888
- 🕐 Casino Complex: 24 hours, seven days
- 🍴 Cafés and restaurants
- 🚇 Flinders Street
- 🚊 Tram 10, 12, 96, 109
- 🚤 Boat tours on the Yarra
- ♿ Moderate
- 🎫 Free
- ➕ Royal Botanic Gardens (► 24), Melbourne City Centre (► 26), Yarra River (► 29), Melbourne Trams (► 33), Victorian Arts Centre (► 36), Melbourne Aquarium (► 40), National Gallery of Victoria (► 41)
- ❓ Guided tours, night viewing and exhibitions

Melburnians have taken a liking to this district and come here in great numbers on weekends to stroll along the Yarra River, shop, dine at restaurants offering choices of cuisine, and try their luck at the nearby Crown Casino.

Southbank This riverside district across from the city centre was once a dingy industrial area covered with warehouses and workshops. Since its redevelopment in the early 1990s, it has become a popular spot for shopping and dining. Many of Melbourne's new attractions are located here, alongside the long-established Victorian Arts Centre and National Gallery of Victoria. Large sculptures line the riverbank and an arched footbridge joins the Southbank complex to the city. On Sundays the international food hall and an arts and crafts market draw the crowds out to enjoy a stroll beside the river.

Crown Entertainment Complex State-of-the-art cinemas, cafés, cabarets and nightclubs make this complex lively, especially on weekends. There are also 17 bars and 35 restaurants with a range of cuisines and many specialist shops and other retail outlets. At night, the five-storey Atrium features a 90-minute, continuous Four Seasons light and sound show, incorporating three large, computerised fountains. Along the promenade, eight columns that overflow with water by day shoot fireballs at night.

Crown Casino Only a short walk from the city centre and Southbank, you can try your luck at pontoon, roulette, poker, *pai gow*, and the Australian favourite, two-up. There are 350 gaming tables and 2,500 gaming machines in nine separate areas.

YARRA RIVER

Because of its murky colour, the serpentine Yarra is known as the river that flows upside down. To the locals the river is the heart and soul of the city. The waterway is perfect for a relaxing cruise and its banks make a great gathering place.

The river The Yarra is not particularly busy along the city centre but you will often see tour boats cruising past and rowers practising their sport. However, there's plenty going on where the river empties into Port Phillip Bay and a good place to absorb the scene is from the Princes Bridge, built in 1888. The best way to experience the river is by tour boat. The down-river cruise includes the Port and Docklands area with its range of new developments. The cruise up the river shows off more natural beauty – lovely parks and gardens, stylish suburban architecture and natural woodlands. Or rent a bicycle in Alexandra Gardens and cycle up or down the river on the excellent bike paths. Picnics on the grassy banks of the Yarra are a Melbourne tradition. To see the Yarra in a natural setting don't miss Studley Park Boathouse at Kew, 6.5km from the city, where you can hire rowing boats and canoes to explore the calm waters at your own pace.

HIGHLIGHTS

- The walkways
- View from the Princes Bridge
- Picnic spots
- River cruises
- Cycleways
- Studley Park Boathouse

INFORMATION

- 21S; 7H
- Melbourne River Cruises, Princes Walk
- 9629 7233
- Daily
- Various
- Walkway: free.
  Boat tours: moderate
- Royal Botanic Gardens (➤ 24), Melbourne City Centre (➤ 26), Southbank and the Crown Complex (➤ 28), Melbourne Cricket Ground (➤ 31), Victorian Arts Centre (➤ 36), Kings Domain (➤ 37), Melbourne Aquarium (➤ 40), National Gallery of Victoria (➤ 41)

Princes Bridge

OLD MELBOURNE GAOL

HIGHLIGHTS

- Bluestone building
- Death masks
- Ned Kelly memorabilia
- Night performances

One of Melbourne's most macabre attractions, this historic bluestone prison is fixed in national folklore as the place where Australia's most famous bushranger was hanged. Here you can see the gallows and the death masks of several unfortunates.

Above: interior of Old Melbourne Gaol

A gruesome past This grim, gloomy place with thick walls, small cells and heavy iron doors is Victoria's oldest surviving penal establishment. To spend some time within its walls is to begin to understand the realities of prison life in the 19th century. Begun in 1841 and completed in 1864, it was designed along the lines of the Pentonville Modern Prison in London and consists of three levels of cells. The gallows, where 135 men and women were hanged, is the centrepiece of the complex. The death masks of some of those executed are on display, along with their stories. The most famous hanging was that of the bushranger Ned Kelly, one of the nation's folk heroes, an outlaw executed in 1889, whose famous last words were, 'Such is life'. A wooden tableau depicts the Kelly execution and nightly performances re-create the prison's gruesome past. The present cell block, the only one remaining from the original prison, was in use until 1929, when the last prisoners were transferred to other prisons; between 1942 and 1946 it was used as a military detention barracks.

Penal Museum Presented as exhibits in many of the cells, the museum provides information on many infamous inmates, displays the Hangman's Box with its original contents, and chronicles incarcerations. The flogging frame is on view along with the punishment instruments.

INFORMATION

- ✛ 20Q
- ✉ Russell Street
- ☎ 9663 7228
- ◷ Daily 9:30–4:30
- 🚋 City Circle Tram
- 🍴 Moderate
- ↔ Melbourne Museum (► 25), Queen Victoria Market (► 27), Melbourne City Centre (► 26), Chinatown (► 43)
- ❓ Tour groups by arrangement

MELBOURNE CRICKET GROUND

Many Melburnians live for sport, especially cricket and their beloved Australian Rules Football. This 100,000-seat arena has long been the epicentre of these two sports in the city and was the focal point of the 1956 Olympics.

The hallowed ground Each week of the season, football followers deck themselves out in their team colours and crowd the stands to support their favourites. If you are in Melbourne from March to September, attend a football match and soak up the atmosphere – few stadiums in the world generate the excitement of the MCG when it is packed. Alternatively, in summer, you can watch cricket. A guided tour is always a must: you can sit in the room where the team watches the game, visit the Long Room hung with portraits of cricketing greats, and inspect the memorabilia-packed Melbourne Cricket Club Museum. For many, a tour highlight is to stand on the famous playing field and try to imagine what it's like when a roaring crowd fills the stands.

Olympic Museum This major International Olympic Committee-endorsed museum traces the history of the modern games. There are photographic displays of each of the modern Olympics, with priceless items of memorabilia such as wild olive branches won at Athens in 1896 and various gold medals. Interactive exhibits allow you to ski a downhill course and score goals at football.

Australian Gallery of Sport Perhaps the best way to learn about cricket and Australian Rules Football is to visit this gallery, in the same complex, which includes the Australian Cricket Hall of Fame and hosts temporary exhibitions.

HIGHLIGHTS

- Standing on the playing field
- Members' Pavilion
- Interactive games
- Olympic Museum
- Australian Gallery of Sport

INFORMATION

- 23T;8H
- Jolimont Street
- 9657 8879
- Daily 9–5
- Tram 48, 75
- Poor
- Moderate
- Royal Botanic Gardens (► 24), Melbourne City Centre (► 26), Southbank and the Crown Complex (► 28), Yarra River (► 29), Victorian Arts Centre (► 36), Kings Domain (► 37), Fitzroy Gardens (► 39), National Gallery of Victoria (► 41)
- Tours depart hourly from the Gallery of Sport foyer, from 10–3 on non-event days

9

BRUNSWICK STREET, FITZROY

- People-watching
- Bric-a-brac shops
- Designer clothes shops
- Nightlife

A casual walk along Fitzroy's lively Brunswick Street with its fascinating people, quirky bazaars and shops, excellent cafés and restaurants, and exciting nightlife provides an entertaining glimpse of an alternative Melbourne.

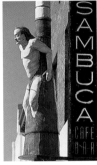

Sculpture in Brunswick Street

Multicultural Once a fashionable residential area just northeast of the city centre, Fitzroy has since gone through phases of working-class and immigrant inhabitants. Today the area is increasingly occupied by some of Melbourne's vibrant subcultures including students and artists, along with trendy, inner-city urbanites attracted by the suburb's eclectic nature. Part of the fun of hanging out here is to sit with a coffee and people-watch. For shopping, the area is hard to beat; it's a great place to buy books, art, antiques, bric-a-brac and the latest retro fashions. Melbourne's Spanish community is based in nearby Johnson Street where you will find specialist eating places, grocery shops and gift shops. You'll also find food of every variety – Turkish, Greek, Italian, Thai, Malaysian and Tibetan – especially around the junction with Johnson Street. There are plenty of restaurants featuring modern Australian cuisine, too. Go for places with a crowd—the local stamp of approval.

INFORMATION

- 22P; 7F
- Brunswick Street, Fitzroy
- Cafés and restaurants
- Tram 11
- Fair
- Chinatown (► 43), Melbourne Museum (► 25), Melbourne City Centre (► 26), Old Melbourne Gaol (► 30), Melbourne trams (► 33)

University of Melbourne Not far away from Brunswick Street is the University of Melbourne, opened in 1855. You can wander around the attractive campus, full of fine college buildings, and visit the excellent library, free museums and galleries. During the academic year, from March to December, there are public lectures and free concerts at lunchtime. Evening concerts are held in the beautifully renovated Melba Hall.

MELBOURNE TRAMS

It would be hard to imagine Melbourne without its trams; since the 1880s this reliable and pleasant form of travel has been the backbone of the public transport system and remains an integral part of the fabric of the city.

A proud history At a time when most cities of the world were dispensing with this efficient means of transport, Melbourne's city planners retained their trams, and today some 314km of double track extend to many of the city's inner suburbs. Quiet, pneumatic models have largely superseded the old rattlers, but many of these wooden-seated old faithfuls, first introduced in the 1880s, still ply the city streets. They can provide an inexpensive tour, particularly the No. 8 to Toorak and the No. 15 to St Kilda. Use the burgundy-coloured, restored W-class trams, known as the City Circle Trams, for a free ride around the edge of the city centre. You can catch these at a several designated spots. Listen for the distinctive bell, and when crossing streets to board, watch out for the traffic, which may not stop for you.

Painted trams Artists have been invited to use the tram carriages as their canvases, so many styles of art can be seen. Other trams carry large, colourful advertisements.

Colonial Tramcar Restaurant Certain trams have become the Colonial Tramcar Restaurants, the only tram restaurants in the world. While cruising the streets of South Yarra, Toorak, St Kilda and South Melbourne, you are treated to Australian cuisine and wine, and great views of the city from a middle-of-the-road perspective. The converted 1920s trams are equipped with stabilsers to ensure a smooth journey. Booking is essential.

HIGHLIGHTS

- Free City Circle Tram
- Inexpensive scenic tours
- Painted trams
- Colonial Tramcar Restaurant

INFORMATION

- ✉ Colonial Tramcar Restaurant departs from Stop 125, Normandy Road, South Melbourne
- ☎ Tram timetable information: 131 638.
  Colonial Tramcar Restaurant: 9696 4000
- 🕐 Colonial Tramcar Restaurant: Daily, early and late dinners; lunches subject to demand
- 🍴 Colonial Tramcar Restaurant
- ♿ Poor
- 💷 Inexpensive to ride.
  Expensive to dine.
- ↔ Royal Botanic Gardens (➤ 24), Queen Victoria Market (➤ 27), Melbourne City Centre (➤ 26), Southbank and the Crown Complex (➤ 28), Yarra River (➤ 29), Rialto Towers Observation Deck (➤ 34), Immigration Museum (➤ 42), Chinatown (➤ 43)

11

RIALTO TOWERS OBSERVATION DECK

HIGHLIGHTS

- View of the Yarra River, the city buildings and south to Port Phillip Bay
- Night views
- Zoom-lens binoculars
- Rialto Vision Theatre

INFORMATION

- 19S
- 525 Collins Street
- 9629 8222
- Sun–Thu 10–10; Fri–Sat 10–11
- Licensed café
- Flinders Street, Spencer Street
- Good
- Moderate
- Melbourne City Centre (➤ 26), Queen Victoria Market (➤ 27), Southbank and the Crown Complex (➤ 28), Yarra River (➤ 29), Melbourne Trams (➤ 33), Melbourne Aquarium (➤ 40), Polly Woodside Maritime Museum (➤ 48)

For the best views in Melbourne, head for the 55th floor of the city's tallest building, where an observation deck provides spectacular 360-degree views. On a clear day you can see out over Port Phillip Bay and northwest to Tullamarine Airport.

The structure The 230-m, 58-level main tower, on Collins Street west, completed in 1986, is the tallest office building in Australia.

The Observation Deck The deck, opened in 1994, has information on Melbourne's history and large photographic displays mounted at all points of the compass showing the names of the most important sights. The purpose-built Rialto Vision Theatre, on the Plaza level, shows a 20-minute movie in a super-wide cinematic format, 'Melbourne, the Living City'.

The views The deck is a great place to get a handle on the city's layout. The 360-degree views are incredible in fine weather – you can even see aircraft taking off and landing at the airport. Powerful zoom-lens binoculars extend your view

and special glass windows ensure glare-free photography, and, being semi-reflective change colour when the sun sets. The café is a good place to warm up after the chilly winds on the outdoor decks. A visit to the deck after dark is a magical experience. The city lights stretch out far and wide and you get a different perspective on the pyrotechnics at the Crown Entertainment Complex.

DANDENONG RANGES

The scenic Dandenongs, about 35km east of the city, have always been Melburnians' favoured summer recreation destination. City dwellers flock here to escape the summer heat and return in the cooler months for bracing mountain walks.

The mountains On a clear day, the Dandenong Ranges can be seen from central Melbourne. Soaring mountain ash forests, glades of tree ferns and mountain streams are all part of the experience in the Dandenongs. The highest point is Mt Dandenong at 633m. Despite the encroachment of the suburbs, there are many opportunities to get off the beaten track. Besides hiking and picnicking, there are magnificent gardens, art and craft shops, nurseries and tearooms to visit.

Puffing Billy Railway Along the southeastern slopes, on the edge of Sherbrooke Forest Park, the narrow-gauge Puffing Billy Railway carries day-trippers from quaint Belgrave, in the foothills, to pretty Emerald Lake Park in the mountains. This is the oldest steam railway in Australia and one of the finest preserved in the world. The winding journey through forests and fern gullies captures the romance and charm of the bygone days of steam.

William Ricketts Sanctuary In this tranquil, 1.6ha wooded area, about 200 half-hidden, kiln-fired, clay sculptures of Aboriginal figures, the work of the talented sculptor William Ricketts (1899–1993), who founded the sanctuary, nestle among mossy rocks and tree ferns. Ricketts lived for many years with the Aboriginal people of Central Australia and evidence of their culture shows through in his work. Concerts are also held here in the summer.

HIGHLIGHTS

- Cool mountain forests
- Puffiing Billy Railway
- Bushwalks
- William Ricketts Sanctuary
- Gardens
- Art and craft shopping

INFORMATION

Puffing Billy Railway
- see GM map
- Old Monbulk Road, Belgrave
- 9754 6800
- Four times daily
- Lunch in VIP carriages
- Good
- Expensive

William Ricketts Sanctuary
- see GM map
- Mt Dandenong Tourist Road, Mt Dandenong
- 131 963
- Daily 10–4:30
- Churinga Café
- Fair
- Moderate

13

VICTORIAN ARTS CENTRE

HIGHLIGHTS

- Elegant spire
- Location on the Yarra River
- Concert Hall
- Artworks
- Theatres Building
- Performing Arts Museum
- Guided tours

INFORMATION

- 21T
- 100 St Kilda Road
- Information: 9281 8000. Ticketmaster: 136 166
- Daily 9–late
- Cafés and bars
- Tram 3, 5, 6, 8
- Good
- Free
- Royal Botanic Gardens (➤ 24), Melbourne City Centre (➤ 26), Southbank and the Crown Complex (➤ 28), Yarra River (➤ 29) Melbourne Trams (➤ 33), Kings Domain (➤ 37) Melbourne Aquarium (➤ 40), National Gallery of Victoria (➤ 41)
- Guided tours, exhibitions, special tours and events. Check local press for current shows

The city's bastion of high culture is dominated by the webbed spire of the Theatres Building. The Melbourne Concert Hall, the Westpac Gallery, the Performing Arts Museum and the Theatres Building are all part of the Arts Centre.

Melbourne Concert Hall This circular building next to the Yarra River is the city's main performing arts venue and home of Opera Australia, the Melbourne Symphony Orchestra and the Australian Ballet. The concert hall features the world's largest stage, a lavish interior, and a large collection of Australian art, and draws performers from around the world.

Theatres Building Linked to the Melbourne Concert Hall by a walkway, this building houses the Playhouse, the State Theatre, the George Fairfax Studio and the Westpac Gallery, which mounts art exhibitions. The Theatres Building is the home of the Melbourne Theatre Company.

Performing Arts Museum The interesting and changing collections found in the foyer display cabinets include theatre costumes, set designs and other memorabilia associated with the performing arts in Melbourne.

KINGS DOMAIN

A major urban green space, the Kings Domain is also home to the Sidney Myer Music Bowl, the cottage of the first governor of Victoria, and the impressive Shrine of Remembrance, a memorial to those who died in World War I.

The park The Alexandra Gardens and Queen Victoria Gardens adjoin the outstanding 36-ha Royal Botanic Gardens, and together form a continuous park between Princes Bridge and South Yarra. Features include monuments to Queen Victoria and King George V, delicate sculptures of women and children, and a floral clock presented to the citizens of Melbourne by the watchmakers of Switzerland in 1966. The popular, open-air Sidney Myer Music Bowl is an impressive venue for both classical and rock concerts.

Shrine of Remembrance At the southern end of the Domain, this imposing memorial commemorates the service men and women of Victoria who died in World War I. The shrine and other nearby memorials – including the cenotaph and eternal flame honouring those who served in World War II, and the Vietnam Memorial – are the focal point for dawn services each year on the national memorial day, Anzac Day. The podium steps give a good view back to the city.

Governor La Trobe's Cottage This pretty little cottage, Victoria's first Government House, was brought from England in 1839 by Charles La Trobe, who became the first Lieutenant-Governor of the young colony. First set up at Jolimont, the building has been relocated and restored by Australia's National Trust, and many of the furnishings are original. The present nearby Government House (➤ 54) is periodically open to the public.

HIGHLIGHTS

- River walk
- Cycle paths
- Monument to Queen Victoria
- Floral Clock
- Sidney Myer Music Bowl
- Shrine of Remembrance
- Governor La Trobe's Cottage
- Government House

INFORMATION

- ✚ 21U; 7H
- ✉ St Kilda Road
- ☎ La Trobe's Cottage and bookings for Government House tours: 9654 5528
- 🕐 Shrine of Remembrance: Daily 10–5
  La Trobe's Cottage: Daily 11–4
- 🚃 Tram 3, 5, 6, 8
- ♿ Good
- 🎟 Free
- ↔ Royal Botanic Gardens (➤ 24), Melbourne City Centre (➤ 26), Southbank and the Crown Entertainment Complex (➤ 28), Yarra River (➤ 29), Melbourne Trams (➤ 33), Victorian Arts Centre (➤ 36), Fitzroy and Treasury Gardens (➤ 39), National Gallery of Victoria (➤ 41)
- ❓ Bicycles for rent

Above: Shrine of Remembrance, Kings Domain

37

15

WERRIBEE MANSION & OPEN RANGE ZOO

HIGHLIGHTS

- Heritage gardens
- Period furnishings
- Italianate architecture
- Farm buildings
- Rose Garden
- Zebras and cheetahs

This splendidly renovated old mansion stands on the banks of the Werribee River, a thirty-minute drive from Melbourne on the way to Geelong. At the nearby Open Range Zoo, African animals live in a natural Australian bush setting.

Open Range Zoo at Werribee Park

INFORMATION

- off GM map to the west
- The Mansion at Werribee, Open Range Zoo and Victoria State Rose Garden, K Road, Werribee
- The Mansion: 131 963. Victoria State Rose Garden: 9742 6717. Open Range Zoo: 9731 9600
- The Mansion: Daily 10–5. Victoria State Rose Garden: Daily 9–5. Open Range Zoo: Daily 9–5
- Café
- Moderate
- Moderate
- Geelong and the Bellarine Peninsula (▶ 20)
- Guided tours/bus tour

The Mansion at Werribee Park Audio headphones and guides in period costume show this imposing, 19th-century example of Australia's pastoral heritage to its best advantage. Constructed between 1874 and 1877, the Italianate mansion is the largest private residence ever built in Victoria. Be sure to stroll around the 10ha of formal grounds, with its ornamental lake and grotto, and explore the restored bluestone farm buildings and orchard.

Victoria State Rose Garden Next to the mansion over 4,000 rose bushes are planted out in the shape of a Tudor rose. You can sit on the edge of the rose garden or picnic on the nearby lawns beneath the cool, shady trees.

Open Range Zoo You can either stroll around the zoo's 200ha at your own pace, or take a 50-minute guided safari around the grassy plains and sweeping river terraces. Giraffes, zebras, antelopes and hippopotamuses roam freely here. Walking trails pass natural enclosures containing cheetahs, monkeys and ostriches.

16

FITZROY & TREASURY GARDENS

The magnificent, tree-lined avenues of the Fitzroy Gardens, designed in 1857, were laid out in the form of a Union Jack flag. A poignant memorial to former US President John F Kennedy is the centrepiece of the nearby Treasury Gardens.

Fitzroy Gardens The Fitzroy Gardens, with partly hidden glades, waterfalls and shady avenues of elms forming canopies across the pathways, is the location of Cook's Cottage. Also within the gardens is the Fairy Tree, whose trunk is carved with fantasy figures and Australian animals, a conservatory, and the miniature Tudor Village which was presented to Melbourne by the people of Lambeth, London, in appreciation of food packages sent to Britain by Melburnians after World War II.

Cook's Cottage This small, typically English cottage dating from 1755, was the home of the parents of the distinguished navigator, Captain James Cook. Dismantled, it was shipped from Yorkshire to Melbourne in 1934 to be erected, stone by stone, on this site in the Fitzroy Gardens. Furnished in the style of the period, it contains an interpretive area that explores the life of James Cook.

Treasury Gardens At lunchtime, many city workers frequent this pleasant, tranquil park planted with poplars, elms, oaks and cedars. There is a memorial to US President John F Kennedy at the edge of the gardens' pretty ornamental lake.

HIGHLIGHTS

- Avenues of trees
- Conservatory
- Fairy Tree
- Model Tudor village
- Cook's Cottage
- John F Kennedy Memorial

INFORMATION

- 22R; 8G
- Off Wellington Parade
- Cook's Cottage: 9658 8713
- Cook's Cottage: Daily 9–5:30
- Restaurant
- Jolimont
- Tram 78, 79
- Moderate
- Royal Botanic Gardens (➤ 24), Melbourne City Centre (➤ 26), Yarra River (➤ 29), Melbourne Trams (➤ 33), Kings Domain (➤ 37), Chinatown (➤ 43)

Cook's Cottage, Fitzroy Gardens

MELBOURNE AQUARIUM

HIGHLIGHTS

- Hand-feeding sharks
- Mangrove and billabong exhibits
- Simulator rides
- Deep sea trench
- Themed retail outlet
- Dive school
- Walk-through tunnels

INFORMATION

- 19T
- Corner of Queens Wharf Road and Kings Way
- 9620 0999
- Daily 9–5
- Snack bar and licensed brasserie
- Spencer Street or Flinders Street
- City Circle Tram
- Very good
- Expensive
- Melbourne City Centre (➤ 26), Southbank and the Crown Complex (➤ 28), Yarra River (➤ 29), Melbourne Trams (➤ 33), Rialto Towers Observation Deck, (➤ 34), Polly Woodside Maritime Museum (➤ 48)

This popular CBD attraction includes a walk-through view of life under the southern oceans and a chance to watch divers hand-feeding sharks and rays. If you're feeling adventurous, join them in the Dive with Sharks programme.

The aquarium Start your visit on the ground floor, where a multitude of tanks highlight the diverse smaller marine creatures. Then walk to first floor and get a close look at the rays and fish in the re-created mangrove ecosystem, and the long-necked turtles and eels in the billabong. The rock pool exhibit, also on this level, has hermit crabs, sea urchins, starfish, sea cucumbers and other creatures that can be handled. Back on the ground level is a huge floor-to-ceiling tank, complete with coral atoll, that contains many Great Barrier Reef invertebrate and fish species.

The oceanarium For an insight into the fantastic inhabitants of the Great Southern Ocean, view the 2.2-million litre Oceanarium from walk-through tunnels and talk to divers as they feed giant sharks and stingrays.

Action stations Those seeking something more exhilarating can board one of three state-of-the-art rollercoaster simulators. Or try the Dive with Sharks programme, if you dare.

NATIONAL GALLERY OF VICTORIA

Australia's foremost art gallery, completed in 1968, has a vast collection of superb international art. The new centre in Federation Square showcases all aspects of Australian art, featuring a unique Aboriginal section.

National collection 'One Vision, Two Galleries' advertises the on-going exciting development of the National Gallery of Victoria (NGV). The existing building in St Kilda Road is undergoing renovation at the time of writing and is due to reopen late in 2002. In the meantime highlights will be displayed at a temporary site in Russell Street at the rear of the State Library. More than 80,000 works of art range from 2,400 BC to the present day, including pre-Colombian artefacts, works by European Old Masters, including Tiepolo and Rembrandt, works by Rodin, Picasso and Henry Moore, American paintings and sculpture, as well as costumes, textiles, furniture and an excellent collection of glass.

Australian art The Ian Potter Centre in Federation Square is the new gallery of the NGV featuring the country's finest collection of Australian art, from early Aboriginal art through to superb exhibits by modern Australian artists including Tom Roberts, Arthur Streeton, Sidney Nolan, Arthur Boyd and Brett Whiteley.

HIGHLIGHTS

- Aboriginal art
- Australian impressionists
- European art
- Sculpture courtyard
- Great Hall ceiling
- Decorative arts

INFORMATION

- 21U
- 180 St. Kilda Road, Melbourne; temporary location, 285 Russell Street
- 9208 0222
- Daily 10–5
- Restaurant and café
- Tram 3, 5, 6, 8
- Excellent
- Free (charges for some exhibitions)
- Royal Botanic Gardens (► 24), Melbourne City Centre (► 26), Southbank and the Crown Complex (► 28), Yarra River (► 29), Melbourne Trams (► 33), Victorian Arts Centre (► 36), Kings Domain (► 37)
- Free tours daily, lectures, films, library and shop

Artwork from the National Gallery of Victoria

41

IMMIGRATION MUSEUM

HIGHLIGHTS

- 'Ship' experience
- The Long Room
- Hellenic Antiquities Museum
- Immigration Discovery Centre

INFORMATION

- 19T
- 400 Flinders Street
- 9927 2700
- Spencer Street or Flinders Street
- City Circle Tram
- Daily 10–5
- Licensed café
- City Circle Tram
- Good
- Moderate
- Melbourne City Centre (► 26), Melbourne Trams (► 33), Rialto Towers Observation Deck (► 34), Melbourne Aquarium (► 40), Polly Woodside Maritime Museum (► 48)

A ship's cabin exhibit at the Immigration Museum

Voices, images, letters and artefacts bring Victoria's immigration history to life in this contemporary museum. The former Customs Service building, renovated in the late 1990s, houses both the Hellenic Antiquities and Immigration museums.

Hardships revisited In this innovative museum special exhibitions sensitively explore themes of departure and arrival, journeys and settlement, and document the effects of immigration on Victoria since the early 1800s. Here you can walk through the re-creation of several ships' cabins and experience the cramped quarters endured by immigrants from the 1850s onwards on their way to Victoria. The Sarah and Baillieu Myer Immigration Discovery Centre has a library that focuses on cultural heritage and immigration, where you can look up information on family history. Outside, at the rear of the museum, is a memorial courtyard bearing the names of immigrants. It's worth a visit for the building alone, which was built between 1858 and 1870. The centrepiece of the museum is the elegant Long Room, a marvellous piece of Renaissance revival architecture, featuring 16 ionic columns and a mosaic tile floor.

Hellenic Antiquities Museum This gallery on the second floor showcases Hellenic antiquities and changing exhibitions of Greek art are always on display. The other end of the floor is dedicated to travelling exhibitions from all over the world.

CHINATOWN

The Chinese community has been settled in bustling Little Bourke Street since the gold-rush days of the 1850s. Today excellent restaurants and specialist shops sit next to herbalists and small shops selling Chinese goods and food.

The back streets Chinese gates and two stone lions mark this distinctive part of Little Bourke Street, between Exhibition and Swanston streets, although it spills over into the adjoining streets and lanes. After the gold rush, many Chinese immigrants opened shops, furniture factories and other businesses here, and some of the 19th-century Victorian buildings commissioned by Chinese businessmen and designed by notable architects of the day still stand. Today, Asian supermarkets, restaurants and cake shops cater for Chinese tastes.

Chinese Museum In this museum in Cohen Place, off Little Bourke Street, there are excellent photographic exhibits and an interesting walk-through re-creation of the history of the Chinese in early Victoria. Among the exhibits is a life-size replica of a Warrior General from the second century BC, the only such replica outside China, and Dai Loong, reputedly the world's longest processional dragon that is paraded by 100 men through the streets each year at the Moomba Festival in March, a 10-day carnival with cultural and sporting events.

HIGHLIGHTS

- Interesting shops; restaurants
- Chinese Museum
- Distinctive architecture

INFORMATION

- ✚ 21Q
- ✉ Little Bourke Street (east). Chinese Museum, 22 Cohen Place
- ☎ Chinese Museum: 9663 1797
- ⏰ Sun–Fri 10–4:30; Sat noon–4:30
- 🍴 Many restaurants
- Ⓟ Parliament
- 🚋 City Circle Tram
- ♿ Moderate
- 🔊 Moderate
- ↔ Royal Botanic Gardens (➤ 24), Melbourne City Centre (➤ 26), Fitzroy and Treasury Gardens (➤ 39), Yarra River (➤ 29), Melbourne Trams (➤ 33), Kings Domain (➤ 37)
- ❓ Free guided/audiovisual tours

Chinatown – New Year Festival parade

21

MUSEUM OF MODERN ART AT HEIDE

HIGHLIGHTS

- Contemporary art
- Audio tour
- Walks
- Sculpture garden

Celebrating the work of Australia's early modernists, this very special museum and its riverbank sculpture gardens were once the stomping ground of a new generation of artists whose aim was nothing short of revolutionising Australian art.

Theoretical Matter *by Neil Taylor*

The gallery Set on the banks of the Yarra River, Heide once belonged to John and Sunday Reed, whose patronage, beginning in the 1930s, nurtured a new generation of outstanding artists. Starting with a run-down dairy farm, the Reeds built a fine contemporary home and created an inspiring environment in which artists could meet and work.

Modern Art Today these buildings house a permanent collection of Australian modernists; paintings by Arthur Boyd, Charles Blackman, Joy Hester, Sidney Nolan, Albert Tucker, Peter Booth and Jenny Watson, and sculptures by Rick Amor and Stephen Killick. The Discover Heide audio tour provides insights into the lives of the artists influenced by the Reeds.

INFORMATION

- 14C
- 7 Templestowe Road, Bulleen
- Museum: 9850 1500.
  Café: 9852 1406
- Tue–Fri 10–5; Sat, Sun 12–5
- Café 10–5, Tue–Sun
- Heidelberg station
- From station, take bus 291
  and alight near the museum
- Good
- Moderate
- Yarra Valley (► 21)
- Audio tour

The garden Stroll around 5ha of grounds and picnic among the contemporary sculptures installed in the grounds and along the riverbank. The rambling park comprises native and European trees and has a well-tended kitchen garden and sculpture gardens running right down to the Yarra River. Or try the restaurant at the entrance to the museum. Temporary exhibitions and events offer perspectives on aspects of Australian art.

Royal Melbourne Zoo

Gorillas get top billing here, but the otters are just as fascinating, as are indigenous marsupials such as kangaroos, koalas and wombats. The platypus, an egg-laying mammal, is also represented, together with much of Australia's unique birdlife.

Background This popular zoo, Australia's oldest and the third oldest in the world, dates back to 1861, when it was established on its present site in Royal Park. Back in the 1850s Australian flora and fauna was viewed with amazement for its weird and wonderful native variety. The Acclimatisation Society was formed to gather together and protect native species, acclimatising them to captivity. They merged with the Zoological Society in 1861 to create the zoo.

Australian fauna Today the zoo exhibits more than 350 animal species from around the world, including all the popular Australian species, most housed in landscaped enclosures. Platypuses caper in the nocturnal display and fur seals glide past in an underwater environment. Even the gorillas have their own rainforest. You can actually walk right through the lions' den, protected by a caged walkway. Sumatran tigers, otters and pygmy hippopotamuses star in the innovative African and Asian zones.

Royal Park The zoo is the focal point of this 180-ha park, a favourite family destination at weekends. There are hockey and netball stadiums here, as well as facilities for cricket, football, tennis and golf. Elsewhere, green open spaces, shady roads, gardens of native plants and groves of smooth eucalyptus trees make you feel far away from busy Melbourne. Look for the memorial cairn to Burke and Wills, commemorating the fateful crossing of the Australian interior in 1860.

HIGHLIGHTS

- Western lowland gorillas
- Sumatran tigers
- Australian mammals
- Butterfly House
- Japanese Garden
- Platypus nocturnal display
- Royal Park

INFORMATION

- 6E
- Elliot Avenue, Parkville
- 9285 9300
- Daily 9–5
- Variety of cafés and kiosks
- Tram 55, 68, City Explorer Bus
- Good
- Moderate
- University of Melbourne (➤ 55)
- Guided tours, special zookeeper presentations and talks

23

RIPPONLEA & COMO HOUSE

HIGHLIGHTS

- Unique architecture
- Original furniture
- Park-like grounds
- Fountain terrace
- Stunning interior decoration

INFORMATION

Ripponlea

- ✚ see GM map
- ✉ 192 Hotham Street, Elsternwick
- ☎ 9523 6095
- ⏰ Tue–Sun 10–5
- 🚋 Tram 67
- 💵 Moderate
- ❓ Guided tours daily

Como House

- ✚ 26X
- ✉ Corner of Williams Road and Lechlade Avenue, South Yarra
- ☎ 9827 2500
- ⏰ Daily 10–5
- 🚋 Tram 8
- 💵 Moderate
- ❓ Guided tours daily

Above: Como House
Below: Ripponlea

Managed by the National Trust, these outstanding examples of 19th-century suburban estates are just a few kilometres apart, south of the Yarra River. Their magnificent gardens are intact and their architecture is very well preserved.

Ripponlea Built between 1868 and 1887 with distinctive polychrome bricks, this lavish, ornate, Romanesque mansion has 36 opulent rooms where Victorian splendour mixes with the 1930s tastes of its last owner. The fine 5.7ha Victorian pleasure garden includes an orchard, a desert garden, an ornamental lake with islands and decorative bridges, and a Victorian fernery.

Como House Two hectares of gardens surround this elegant home, built between 1840 and 1859, in an unusual mix of Australian Regency and Italianate styles. This gracious building perfectly exemplifies what wealthy landowners built for themselves in mid 19th-century Australia. The kitchen outbuilding dates from the 1840s, and the original laundry and some furnishings also remain. Sloping lawns, walks among flower gardens, and pine and cypress glades make up the grounds; there's also a croquet lawn, a fountain terrace and a water garden by 19th-century landscape designer Eliss Stones.

St Kilda

Feel the sand under your feet at the city's favourite bayside beach or take a walk along the Esplanade and pier to work up an appetite for a meal in one of the area's many restaurants. For cakes and pastries, a visit to nearby Acland Street is a must.

The beach Since Melbourne's early days people have flocked to this beachside suburb, 6.5km southeast of the city, to enjoy the cool sea breezes off Port Phillip Bay. Late in the 19th century, the wealthy built large houses in the area, away from the heat of the city. Rail services and motor vehicles soon put other suburbs within reach, and in St Kilda many mansions were demolished or turned into boarding houses.

The streets Now, post-gentrification, the area is a hive of stylish activity, and Fitzroy and Acland streets are a mix of retail and dining establishments, lively bars and art galleries. Many of the grand old buildings have been restored and the charm of the place is immense. On Sundays an open-air arts and crafts market along the Esplanade draws crowds. Nearby Luna Park (▶ 56), established in 1912, is one of St Kilda's best-known landmarks. Although the fun park opens only on weekends and public holidays, its rides still attract the young and young at heart.

St Kilda Pier This popular pier, erected in 1857, is about 150m from the beach end of Fitzroy Street and two blocks northwest of Luna Park. From the café and marina at the end of the pier, you can see the grand sweep of the bay around to Port Melbourne. Walkways have been constructed along the shoreline and the foreshore has been landscaped. The beaches are fine for swimming although there can be an undertow. Windsurfing is popular.

Café scene in St Kilda

HIGHLIGHTS

- Swimming in summer
- Cafés on Fitzroy Street and Acland Street
- Patisseries
- Walking on the pier or along the beach
- Luna Park
- St Kilda Botanical Gardens
- Nightlife

INFORMATION

✚	7L
✉	St Kilda
☎	Visitor Information: 132 842
◷	24 hours daily
🍴	Many good cafés and restaurants
🚌	Bus 16 from Swanston Street
♿	Generally good
💲	Free
↔	St Kilda Bay walking trail (▶ 16), Luna Park (▶ 56)
❓	Frequent festivals, exhibitions and events

25

POLLY WOODSIDE MARITIME MUSEUM

HIGHLIGHTS

- Polly Woodside
- Maritime exhibits
- Ship models
- Old dry dock

INFORMATION

- 18U
- Lorimer Street East, Southbank
- 9699 9760
- Daily 10–4
- Café
- Flinders Street
- Tram 12, 96, 109
- Poor
- Moderate
- Melbourne City Centre (➤ 26), Queen Victoria Market (➤ 27), Southbank and the Crown Complex (➤ 28), Yarra River (➤ 29), Melbourne Trams (➤ 33), Rialto Towers Observation Deck (➤ 34), Melbourne Aquarium (➤ 40), Chinatown (➤ 43)
- Tours daily

Founded on immigration and trade, Melbourne has a rich maritime history. The classic, beautifully restored barque, **Polly Woodside***, moored afloat in an original dry dock, symbolises the aspirations of the city's earliest European settlers.*

Polly Woodside The centrepiece of this maritime museum on the riverfront near Spencer Street Bridge is the *Polly Woodside*, an iron-hulled, three-masted barque built in Belfast in 1885. Plying the South American run, she sailed around Cape Horn 16 times as a coal and nitrate carrier. Rechristened *Rona*, the ship sailed the Tasman and Pacific Oceans between 1904 and 1924, when she was converted to a coal hulk for use in Port Melbourne. Restoration by volunteers began in 1968 and now you can board this majestic reminder of Australia's maritime past. The ship is moored in the Dukes and Orrs Dry Dock, built in 1875. Nearby is the dock's original steam-powered pump and pump house.

The museum An old cargo shed in the grounds houses maritime relics, models of ships and old film footage and photographs that show the origins of Melbourne's port. Displays illustrate the importance of trade in the founding of the colony of Victoria. A souvenir shop and kiosk are attached to the museum. Around the grounds are a floating lighthouse, small boats and equipment and a workshop where keen volunteers mend sails and rebuild parts of the ship.

Above: Polly Woodside
Right: On deck, Polly Woodside

MELBOURNE's
best

49

THE GREAT OUTDOORS

See Top 25 Sights for
DANDENONG RANGES (► 35)
FITZROY & TREASURY GARDENS (► 39)
KINGS DOMAIN (► 37)
ROYAL BOTANIC GARDENS (► 24)
ST KILDA (► 47)
ROYAL PARK (► 45)
YARRA RIVER (► 29)

Adventure activities

In Melbourne you can hike, dive, windsurf, sail and even go abseiling on the cliffs. Details of operators are available from the Victorian Tourism Information Service (☎ 132 842).
Cliffhanger, Australia's tallest and most sophisticated indoor rock climbing facility, is at Altona North (☎ 9369 6400).
Urban Extreme runs white-water rafting, caving, hiking and other tours (☎ 9490 1456).

BRISBANE RANGES NATIONAL PARK
If you are travelling to Geelong (► 20) and points west, consider a detour to Bacchus Marsh and this mountain park, which has many good walking trails. The prime attraction is the picnic area at Anakie Gorge, where you may spot koalas in the trees. The return journey from Geelong could follow the Princes Freeway before diverting to the Open Range Zoo at Werribee (► 38).

✚ off GM map to west ✉ Geelong and Great Ocean Road Visitor Centre ☎ 5275 5797 🕐 Daily 9–5 🍴 Picnic area 💲 Free

FRENCH ISLAND
Once a prison farm, this undeveloped island is as close as Melbourne gets to wilderness with its prolific koala colony, the rare potoroo, and 234 species of birds that include ground-breeding muttonbirds. There are also possibilities for hiking and cycling.

✚ off GM map to south ✉ Peninsula Visitor Centre ☎ 5987 3078 🕐 Daily 9–5 🍴 At the Lodge ⛴ Ferry from Stony Point 💲 Moderate

Little penguin nesting on Phillip Island

MACEDON RANGES

Cool mountain air, great scenery and the landmark features of Hanging Rock lure visitors to this area, along with trails for mountain hiking, tranquil private and public gardens, excellent restaurants, wineries and hundreds of bed-and-breakfasts. It's a little over an hour's drive from Melbourne.

off GM map to north ⊠ Woodend Visitor Information Centre ☎ 5427 2033 ⊙ Daily 9–5 🍴 Restaurant; picnic areas 🖐 Moderate

PHILLIP ISLAND

On the island's Summerland Beach you can view an amazing colony of little penguins and the so-called Penguin Parade. Spotlights illuminate these engaging birds as they return to their nesting burrows in the evening. The island has a substantial population of waterbirds, a good wildlife sanctuary, and the Koala Conservation Centre with a visitor area and elevated boardwalks through the bush. You can swim and dive in the calm waters of the many protected bays and beaches.

off GM map to south ⊠ Phillip Island Information Centre ☎ 5956 7447 ⊙ Daily 9–5 🍴 Restaurants; picnic areas 🖐 Moderate

WILSONS PROMONTORY

The Bass Strait laps at the Promontory, 200km southeast of Melbourne, on three sides. The coastal scenery is superb and a network of walking trails enables you to take in the flora and fauna. Besides beaches and cliffs, there are immense outcrops of granite, coastal heathland and fern gullies.

off GM map to south ☎ 131 963 ⊙ Daily 🍴 Picnic facilities 🖐 Moderate

YARRA RANGES NATIONAL PARK

Stretching from mountain tops to rivers, this park protects the forested water catchments that supply Melbourne's water. Included are sub-alpine heathlands, snow gum woodlands, alpine and mountain ash forests, and cool temperate rainforests. The most accessible part of the park from Melbourne is Badger Weir, where you can picnic, walk and maybe spot a lyrebird displaying its distinctive long tail feathers.

off GM map to north ⊠ Healesville Visitor Information Centre ☎ 5962 2600 ⊙ Daily 9–5 🍴 Picnic facilities 🖐 Free

YOU YANGS REGIONAL PARK

From the Bellarine Peninsula (➤ 20) it is possible to make a short diversion to this park, a scenic range of volcanic hills not far from the Princes Freeway. The highest point in the park is Flinders Peak, with great views across Port Phillip Bay and Geelong.

off GM map to west ☎ 131 963 ⊙ Daily all hours 🍴 Picnic facilities 🖐 Free

Surfing the Peninsula

The closest surfing beaches to Melbourne are on the Mornington Peninsula. Classic right-handers are to be found at beaches around the town of Flinders, particularly in autumn and winter. Between Flinders and Cape Schanck waves are patchy, but the coast towards Point Nepean has some great spots, including Gunamatta, Ocean Beach and Spooks.

51

GALLERIES & MUSEUMS

Window detail, Gold Treasury Museum

Commercial art galleries

Melbourne has the largest number of commercial art galleries in Australia. A good way to see many of these is to visit the arts precincts in Armadale, St Kilda, Richmond or Fitzroy. Flinders Lane in the city also has many contemporary art galleries. Some galleries worth checking out include: William Mora Gallery (✉ 31 Flinders Lane); Robert Lindsay Gallery (✉ 45 Flinders Lane); and Anna Schwartz Gallery (✉ 185 Flinders Lane).

See Top 25 Sights for
IMMIGRATION MUSEUM (➤ 42)
MUSEUM OF MODERN ART AT HEIDE (➤ 44)
MELBOURNE MUSEUM (➤ 25)
NATIONAL GALLERY OF VICTORIA (➤ 41)
POLLY WOODSIDE MARITIME MUSEUM (➤ 48)

AUSTRALIAN CENTRE FOR CONTEMPORARY ART

The ACCA was founded in 1984 to stimulate, identify and articulate new ideas about current visual culture and act as a site of exploration and discovery, where artists, their work and the public could meet. Changing exhibitions include solo and group shows across all contemporary media. Lectures, forums, performances and screenings addressing current issues are also presented.

✚ 22W ✉ Dallas Brooks Drive, South Yarra ☎ 9654 6422 🕐 Tue–Fri 11–5; Sat, Sun noon–5 🚋 Tram 8 💲 Free

GOLD TREASURY MUSEUM

This superb example of neo-classical architecture, one the the city's finest buildings, was built between 1858 and 1862 as the repository for the young colony's gold reserves. Now a museum, it showcases the wealth of the goldrush era and presents diverse exhibitions highlighting the city's history. It is next door to the pleasant Treasury Gardens.

✚ 21R ✉ Spring Street ☎ 9651 2233 🕐 Mon–Fri 9–5; Sat, Sun 10–4 🚋 City Circle Tram 💲 Moderate

JEWISH MUSEUM OF AUSTRALIA

Dedicated to the conservation, preservation and exhibition of Jewish heritage, arts, customs and religious practices, this museum presents the Australian–Jewish experience. Permanent exhibitions use state-of-the-art interactive displays to explain the Jewish year, belief and ritual, and there's a timeline of Jewish history. The museum also hosts lectures and changing exhibitions.

✚ 8L ✉ 26 Alma Road, St Kilda ☎ 9534 0083 🕐 Tue–Thu 10–4; Sun 11–5 🚋 Tram 3, 67 💲 Moderate

MONTSALVAT

This amazing group of buildings was hand-crafted between 1934 and the 1970s, using mud brick, stone, hewn timbers and slate building materials recycled from some of Melbourne's fine old buildings. It is worth visiting for its eclectic architecture alone. The complex houses a working art colony with artists and craftspeople selling their wares. Music festivals, poetry readings and a range of other activities are held here.

✚ see GM map ✉ Hillcrest Avenue, Eltham ☎ 9439 8771 🕐 Daily 9–5 🚂 Train to Eltham, then Woodridge bus 💲 Moderate

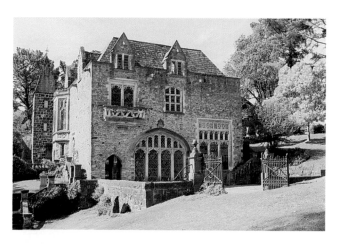

Montsalvat at Eltham

RAILWAY MUSEUM

Operated by the Australian Railway Historical Society, this museum displays 25 locomotives powered by steam, diesel and electricity, plus other items of rolling stock including wagons, carriages and cranes. A photographic display, a replica of an old railway station and other items of railway equipment put the collection in context. There are miniature steam-train rides for children. It's part of the Newport Rail Workshops on Champion Road.

✚ see GM map ✉ Champion Road, North Williamstown ☎ 9596 3249 🕐 Sat, Sun noon–5 💷 Moderate 🚉 North Williamstown

VICTORIAN ARTISTS SOCIETY

The oldest art society in Australia, the charming VAS was founded in 1870 and held its first exhibition in the present galleries. The lovely centre staircase leads to upper galleries. There are always selling exhibitions of paintings, drawings and sculpture by contemporary artists.

✚ 22Q ✉ 430 Albert Street, East Melbourne ☎ 9662 1484 🕐 Daily 10–4:30; Sat, Sun 1:30–4:30 🚋 Tram 11, 109 💷 Free

VICTORIAN TAPESTRY WORKSHOP

Established in 1976, this is one of the world's great tapestry workshops. The weavers here are all artists in their own right and you can watch them at work. Several tapestries are usually being woven at once and the designs have been created by some of Australia's foremost artists. The light, airy Victorian building was a large retail shop during the 1800s.

✚ 19X ✉ 260 Park Street, South Melbourne ☎ 9699 7885 🕐 Mon–Sat 🚋 Tram 1 💷 Moderate

Commercial craft galleries

If you are interested in crafts, visit the markets at St Kilda and the Victorian Arts Centre on Sundays; or stroll down Brunswick Street, Fitzroy, where some of the shops and galleries specialise in crafts. Commercial galleries include Potoroo (✉ Upper Level, Southgate); Makers Mark (✉ 101 Collins Street); and Koorie Connections (✉ 155 Victoria Street).

ARCHITECTURE & INTERIORS

See Top 25 Sights for
CHINATOWN (► 43)
QUEEN VICTORIA MARKET (► 27)
MELBOURNE CITY CENTER (► 26)
MELBOURNE MUSEUM (► 25)
OLD MELBOURNE GAOL (► 30)
RIPPONLEA & COMO HOUSE (► 46)
VICTORIAN ARTS CENTRE (► 36)

Government House and city skyline

Gateway to Melbourne

In Melbourne's new citylink motorway, an extension of the main airport road, local architects Denton Corker Marshall have provided the city with a dramatic and colourful entrance. The innovative design is a pleasant distraction for drivers used to the urban blight of most motorways and a modernist statement by the architects who are also responsible for the striking design of the Melbourne Museum (► 25).

ANZ GOTHIC BANK
This highly decorated Gothic revival bank, completed in 1887, has been compared to the Doge's Palace in Venice. Its magnificent interior, with gold leaf ornamentation amid graceful arches and pillars, features decorative shields from the countries and cities around the world that the original bank, the England, Scottish and Australian Bank, traded with.
🚩 19S ✉ 386 Collins Street ☎ 9273 5555 🕓 Mon–Fri 9:30–4
🚊 City Circle Tram 💷 Free

GOVERNMENT HOUSE
Set within quiet gardens, with the city skyline visible above the trees, this mansion was built in 1876 as the official residence of the Governor of Victoria. The interior is magnificently furnished and the ballroom is larger than the one at Buckingham Palace in London.
🚩 22V ✉ Dallas Brooks Drive ☎ Tours: 9654 5528 🕓 Mon, Wed, Sat 11AM 🍴 Observatory Gate Café 🚊 Tram 3, 6, 8 💷 Moderate

PRINCESS THEATRE
One of the world's grand old theatres, this study in Victorian splendour was built as a palace for the arts in 1854, a time when live theatre was the greatest of

attractions. Today it mounts major musical
productions.

🏛 21Q ✉ 163 Spring Street ☎ 9663 3300 🕐 Daily 🍴 Café
🚋 City Circle Tram 💵 Free

ST PATRICK'S CATHEDRAL

You can see the graceful spires of this bluestone
Catholic cathedral, built in 1897, from many points in
the city. The interior has soaring, slender pillars,
large, stained glass
windows and mosaic floor
tiles. Exquisite glass
mosaics, made in Venice,
are set into the marble and
alabaster altars.

🏛 22Q 🏛 Cathedral Place
☎ 9662 2233 🕐 Mon–Fri 7–6;
Sat, Sun 8–7:30 🚋 Tram 9,12 from
Collins St 💵 Free

Parliament House, Spring Street

ST PAUL'S CATHEDRAL

With its lofty spires and
towers, beautiful
stonework and magnificent
stained glass, this Anglican
cathedral is a classic
example of Gothic revival
architecture from the late
19th century. Inside you
will see carved cedar
woodwork, tessellated tiled floors and detailed,
banded stonework.

🏛 20S ✉ Corner of Swanston and Flinders streets ☎ 9650 3791
🕐 Daily 🚋 City Circle Tram 💵 Free

STATE PARLIAMENT HOUSE

Built during the gold rush in 1856, and amended with
a wide flight of bluestone steps and towering Doric
columns in 1892, this grand building was the first
home of the Australian Parliament, until it moved to
Canberra in 1927. You can attend a session when the
State Parliament is sitting, and there are daily tours.

🏛 21R ✉ Spring Street ☎ 9651 8568 🕐 Tours: Mon–Fri 10–3
🚋 City Circle Tram 💵 Free

UNIVERSITY OF MELBOURNE

Wander around these attractive grounds and admire
the buildings, including Ormond College (1879) with
its gothic tower, and Newman College, designed by
Walter Burley Griffin, in 1918, the architect
responsible for Canberra, the purpose-built, architect-
designed administrative capital of Australia.

🏛 19M;6F ✉ Grattan Street, Parkville ☎ Media Office: 9344 4000
🕐 Daily 🍴 Several cafés 🚋 Tram 1, 3 💵 Free

Windsor Hotel

A Melbourne landmark listed by
the National Trust and the
grandest hotel in Australia, the
meticulously restored Windsor has
all the elegance of a luxury 19th-
century hotel. Even if you don't
stay here, be sure to pop in to
admire the sweeping, wrought-
iron staircase, the ornately
detailed foyer and the rich detail
of the Grand Ballroom. It's in
Spring Street, just opposite the
State Parliament House.

55

FOR CHILDREN

Luna Park

See Top 25 Sights for
MELBOURNE AQUARIUM (► 40)
MELBOURNE MUSEUM (► 25)
MELBOURNE TRAMS (► 33)
OPEN RANGE ZOO (► 38)
POLLY WOODSIDE MARITIME MUSEUM (► 48)
PUFFING BILLY RAILWAY (► 35)
ROYAL MELBOURNE ZOO (► 45)

Australian wildlife

Australia's unique wildlife is always a top attraction. Wildlife parks and zoos offer the chance to see the native fauna, much of which is housed in natural surroundings. Sometimes the easiest way to reach suburban wildlife parks is on an organised tour (► 19).

Wildlife Wonderland

This popular centre incorporates the Giant Earthworm Museum, Wombat World, Koala Haven, Kangaroo Centre and the Great White Shark display.

➕ off GM map to south ✉ Bass Highway, Bass ☎ 5678 2222 ⓒ Daily 9–5:30

ASHCOMBE MAZE

Lose yourself for a while in the rose maze, the first of its kind in the world, and in Australia's oldest and largest hedge maze. Planted in 1980, they were both opened to the public in 1985. Wander among 1,200 rose bushes composed of 217 rose varieties, or stroll around 12ha of theme gardens, including the English-style woodland garden and the Italian-inspired potted garden.

➕ off GM map to south ✉ Red Hill Road, Shoreham, Mornington Peninsula ☎ 5989 8387 ⓒ Daily 10–5 🍴 Licensed café; tearooms 🚌 Bus tour 💲 Moderate

GUMBUYA PARK

Allow at least a day to enjoy these 170ha of natural bushland an hour from Melbourne. View the resident native wildlife – kangaroos, wallabies, wombats and emus – and explore the trails. Rides include a mini-car circuit, mini-motorbikes and jet skis. There's also a mini-golf course and you can cool off on the water slides.

➕ off GM map to west ✉ Princes Highway, Tynong North ☎ 5629 2613 ⓒ Daily 10–6 🍴 Café; picnic areas 🚌 Bus tour 💲 Expensive

HEALESVILLE SANCTUARY

This sanctuary in the Yarra Valley, 60km from Melbourne, displays more than 200 native species, including kangaroos, emus, koalas, wombats, dingoes and platypuses in surroundings as near natural as possible. Here you can learn about the animals from their keepers as they go on their daily rounds. There are also walk-through aviaries, a wetlands walkway and a nocturnal house.

➕ off GM map to north ✉ Badger Creek Road, Healesville ☎ 5957 2800 ⓒ Daily 9–5 🍴 Café; picnic areas 🚌 Bus tour 💲 Moderate

LUNA PARK

This St Kilda institution, built in 1912, is one of the oldest amusement parks in the world. The distinctive entrance in the form of a laughing face has welcomed generations, and the carousel that dates back to the park's earliest days remains a great favourite.

➕ 7L ✉ Lower Esplanade, St Kilda South ☎ 9525 5033 ⓒ Fri 7–11PM; Sat 1–11PM; Sun 1–dusk 🍴 Food stalls 🚋 Tram 16 💲 Moderate

Scienceworks

SCIENCEWORKS MUSEUM

Opened in 1992, this hands-on science and technology museum is an exciting showcase of scientific endeavour's past, present and future. At the adjacent Spotswood Pumping Station, which is listed by the National Trust and is part of the museum, gigantic old steam pumps are on display, and in the Melbourne Planetarium digital technology takes you on a high-speed trip through the universe.

🚌 3H ✉ Booker Street, Spotswood ☎ 9392 4800 🕐 Daily 10–4:30 🍴 Café 🚉 Spotswood Station ⛴ Ferry from Southbank 💷 Moderate

SEAL ROCKS SEA LIFE CENTRE

This high-tech complex stands on the bluff overlooking Seal Rocks, where as many as 12,000 fur seals gather every year to breed. Instantaneous telecasts, which you view in the Panoramic Theatre, show you their activities. You can also take a fascinating 3-D audiovisual ride through space and time, to hear the history of Seal Rocks and see a hologram of a great white shark, the seals' ferocious predator.

🚌 off GM map to south ✉ Penguin Reserve, Cowes ☎ 5952 9333 🕐 Daily 10–dusk 🍴 Restaurants 🚌 Bus tour 💷 Expensive

SOVEREIGN HILL

Employees dress in period costume at this excellent re-creation of an 1850s gold town. You can walk the main streets, shop, go to the theatre, watch craftspeople at work and pan for gold. The entrance fee includes a guided underground mine tour and entry to the Gold Museum.

🚌 off GM map to north ✉ Corner of Main Road and Bradshaw Street, Ballarat ☎ 5331 1944 🕐 Daily 10–5 🍴 Restaurants 🚌 Bus tour 💷 Expensive

Beaches for kids

Many of Melbourne's surfing beaches are not suitable for younger children, so if you are visiting in summer, head for sheltered spots on Port Phillip Bay, such as Brighton, St Kilda and Sandringham. Swim only near designated areas and always where there are other people around. Alternatives to the beaches are the City Baths, a public swimming pool at 420 Swanston Street, and the Melbourne Sports and Aquatic Centre at Albert Road, Albert Park; both are open daily. Remember the Australian sun is fierce, so (to quote Australia's public health warning), slip on a shirt, slop on some Factor15+ sunscreen, and slap on a hat.

Sovereign Hill

VIEWS

The best views in town

To appreciate Melbourne's spectacular surroundings with 360-degree panoramic views, take the high-speed lift to the Rialto Towers Observation Deck (► 34). Open 10am until late, 7 days a week (☎ 9629 8222). If your idea of excitement is floating over Melbourne in a wicker basket, then let Balloon Sunrise take you on an early morning balloon flight, followed by a champagne breakfast (► 82) (☎ 9427 7596).

ARTHURS SEAT

Climb aboard a scenic chairlift and glide at treetop level to the summit of Arthurs Seat for panoramic scenic views of Port Phillip Bay and beyond. At the top there are walking trails, craft galleries and a viewing tower.

➕ off GM to south ✉ Arthurs Seat Road, Dromana ☎ 5987 2565 🍴 Restaurants and cafés 🎟 Moderate

CAPE SCHANCK

Superb views of rugged coastal scenery are available from this lighthouse built in 1859. The complex includes an information centre, a kiosk and a small museum.

➕ off GM map to south ✉ Cape Schanck Road, Cape Schanck ☎ 5988 6251 🍴 Kiosk 🎟 Free

FLAGSTAFF GARDENS

In the early days, the high sloping ground made the area an ideal place to watch ships coming into Port Phillip Bay. The gardens were once a signalling station complete with a flagpole and a burial ground for the early settlers. Laid out in 1840 and one of the city's oldest gardens, these have been landscaped with a variety of indigenous and introduced trees and flowers.

➕ 18Q ✉ Bordered by King, William and La Trobe streets, West Melbourne 🍴 Restaurants nearby 🚋 City Circle Tram 🎟 Free

Port Phillip Bay

INTERESTING SUBURBS

See Top 25 Sights for
FITZROY (➤ 32)
ST KILDA (➤ 47)

CARLTON
This suburb, close to Melbourne University, is the city's Little Italy. Its epicentre is Lygon Street, a 10-minute walk north of the Central Business District (CBD) via Russell Street, where you'll find art cinemas, bookshops, galleries, great cafés and restaurants, and plenty of interesting shops. Nearby Cardigan and Drummond streets have some fine Victorian architecture.

✚ 20P; 7F ✉ Lygon Street, Rathdowne Street 🍴 Many cafés and restaurants 🚊 Tram 1, 22

RICHMOND
In Richmond, one of the city's oldest suburbs and only a short tram ride from the CBD, you can find fashion outlets, with designer seconds, and some great Greek food. Vietnamese culture thrives on Victoria Street, Melbourne's Little Saigon, with unique aromas and exotic dishes.

✚ 25T; 9H ✉ Bridge Road, Swan Street and Victoria Street 🍴 Many cafés and restaurants 🚊 Tram 48, 75

SOUTH YARRA AND PRAHRAN
One of the city's smartest areas, this is the place to go for designer clothing, antiques, fine art, classy restaurants and people-watching. Explore Toorak Road and Chapel Street to get a sense of the place.

✚ 24X; 8J ✉ Toorak Road, Chapel Street 🍴 Many cafés and restaurants 🚊 Tram 8, 72

WILLIAMSTOWN
A visit to this bayside suburb, best reached by the Westgate Bridge or by a ferry from seaside St Kilda, makes an excellent day trip. Shipping docks, moored yachts and boat chandlers all contribute to the maritime atmosphere. Walk along the Strand to take in the arts and crafts shops, and check out the back streets with their clothing and gift shops, small restaurants and interesting old buildings.

✚ 3K ✉ The Strand, The Marina 🍴 Many cafés and restaurants 🚢 Southbank

Bayside beaches
St Kilda (➤ 47) isn't the only bayside beach that's near the city, yet full of greenery. In Brighton, one of the most popular bayside suburbs, the beach is lined with brightly-painted bathing boxes (small changing huts). From there to Beaumaris are 19km of shoreline, with the coastal villages of Black Rock and Sandringham along the way.

View of Melbourne from Williamstown Strand

WHAT'S FREE

Exhibition Building

Built for the 1888 Great Exhibition, this grand, beautifully restored Victorian building in Carlton Gardens is now affiliated to the Melbourne Museum and continues to host trade shows and exhibitions (☎ 9275 5000).

CARLTON GARDENS

These gardens, also known as the Exhibition Gardens, are well laid out with public art, a huge fountain and avenues of mature trees. In the centre is the Royal Exhibition Building, built for the Great Exhibition of 1888, and still used for trade shows. Next to Carlton Gardens, in Nicholson Street, is a restored row of bluestone terrace houses, known as Royal Terrace. The innovative Melbourne Museum is next to the gardens to the north.

➕ 21N; 7F ✉ Between Rathdowne and Nicholson streets 🚋 City Circle Tram 🎟 Free

Flinders Street Station

FLINDERS STREET STATION

Built in 1899, in elaborate Victorian style, this multi-coloured building, with a copper-domed roof and familiar clock, is the hub of suburban rail services. It is famous for its wall of clocks, which give the times of departing trains; 'under the clocks' is a popular meeting place. The surrounding area has many of the city sights and plenty of shops to explore. Just over the Princes Bridge is the Southbank and the Crown Entertainment Complex (► 28).

➕ 20S ✉ Corner of Swanston and Flinders streets ☎ 136 196 ⏰ Daily 🍴 Many eating places 🚉 Flinders Street 🎟 Free

STATE LIBRARY OF VICTORIA

This large library complex with an impressive, domed reading room, is an attraction in its own right. There are changing exhibitions and a vast collection of books that can be browsed through on request.

➕ 20Q ✉ Swanston and Russell streets ☎ 9669 9888 ⏰ Mon–Thu 10–9pm; Thu–Sun 10–6. Closed public hols 🚋 City Circle Tram 🎟 Free

VICTORIA POLICE MUSEUM

An integral part of the Police Historical Unit, this museum preserves old police records, photographs and artefacts from the 1800s. The museum reflects the diversity of work carried out by Victoria Police since the department was established in 1854 and displays period crime paraphernalia.

➕ 18T ✉ 637 Flinders Street ☎ 9247 5216 ⏰ Mon–Fri 10–4 🚋 City Circle Tram 🎟 Free

MELBOURNE
where to...

CONTEMPORARY CUISINE

Prices

The following are per person for two courses, without alcohol, coffee or tips.

£	A$10–20
££	A$21–44
£££	A$45–90

Eating out in Melbourne

It has been said that you can eat your way around the world in Melbourne, and with more than 4,000 restaurants, it may well be Australia's culinary capital. Immigrants have always influenced local tastes. In the past, Europeans set the standards, but today it is Asian chefs, more particularly Vietnamese and Thai, who are affecting what people eat. Restaurants are either licensed or BYO – bring your own alcoholic beverages. Most have a non-smoking area and some have banned smoking entirely – check if smoking is allowed when making a reservation.

ARC (££)

Interesting dishes attract diners to this cosy restaurant with friendly staff providing a good service.

21N ✉ 160 Rathdowne Street, Carlton ☎ 9349 3933 🕒 Lunch and dinner: Tue–Sat 🚃 Tram 96

BECCO (££–£££)

Trendsetters favour this elegant restaurant which specialises in modern Italian fare.

21R ✉ 11–25 Crossley Street, Melbourne ☎ 9663 3000 🕒 Lunch: Mon–Fri. Dinner: daily 🚃 Tram 86, 96

BLAKES (£££)

The chef at this Melbourne institution, where Asia meets the Mediterranean, is not afraid to experiment. Modern decor and cool ambience are a bonus.

20T ✉ Southgate, Southbank (short walk from city centre) ☎ 9699 4100 🕒 Lunch and dinner: daily

BONUM (££–£££)

Everything here is of superb quality, from the service and decor, to the menu of Australian-refined international dishes.

21R ✉ 2 Collins Street, Melbourne ☎ 9650 9387 🕒 Lunch: Mon–Fri. Dinner: Mon–Sat 🚃 City Circle Tram

CIRCA (£££)

In its short lifespan this restaurant has achieved near perfection with its attention to detail, discreet service, elegant setting, and innovative modern British food. It's also pricey.

7L ✉ 2 Acland Street, St Kilda ☎ 9534 5033 🕒 Lunch and dinner: daily 🚃 Tram 16

DONOVANS (££–£££)

This St Kilda favourite, in a good beachside location, serves Mediterranean dishes with a modern twist.

7L ✉ 40 Jacka Boulevard, St Kilda ☎ 9534 8221 🕒 Lunch: Mon–Fri. Dinner: daily 🚃 Tram 16

EST EST EST (£££)

If you are prepared to experiment you are in for a treat at this place, which boasts modern British cuisine and a fine wine list.

7J ✉ 440 Clarendon Street, South Melbourne ☎ 9682 5688 🕒 Lunch and dinner: Mon–Sat 🚃 Tram 12

GUERNICA (££)

Modern Asian-influenced food is the focus here. Its funky location attracts an interesting clientele who appreciate the reasonable prices.

22N ✉ 257 Brunswick Street, Fitzroy ☎ 9416 0969 🕒 Lunch: Sun–Fri. Dinner: daily 🚃 Tram 11

HAIRY CANARY (£–££)

This trendy place is noisy and not the venue for intimate dinner for two, but the fine, modern Mediterranean fare is inspired.

20R ✉ 212 Little Collins Street, Melbourne ☎ 9654 2471 🕒 Lunch and dinner: daily 🚃 City Circle Tram

LANGTON'S (££–£££)

Near the top of the list of Melbourne's best, this stunning classic European restaurant has extremely interesting modern continental dishes and a top-knotch wine list.

➕ 21S ✉ 61 Flinders Lane, Melbourne ☎ 9663 0222
🕐 Lunch: Mon–Fri. Dinner: Mon–Sat 🚋 City Circle Tram

LE RESTAURANT (£££)

Using a variety of Australian produce to superb effect, this excellent hotel restaurant serves up European fare with flair.

➕ 21R ✉ Level 35, Hotel Sofitel, 25 Collins Street
☎ 9653 0000 🕐 Dinner: Tue–Sat 🚋 City Circle Tram

MECCA (££–£££)

Diners flock to this stylish place for the menu of dishes inspired by the cuisine of the Middle East.

➕ 20T ✉ Mid-level, Southgate, Southbank (short walk from city centre) ☎ 9682 2999
🕐 Lunch and dinner: daily

POMME (£££)

Unusual modern British dishes are the focal point at this restaurant, and attention to detail is a hallmark.

➕ 8J ✉ 37 Toorak Road, South Yarra ☎ 9820 9606
🕐 Lunch: Sun–Fri. Dinner: daily 🚋 Tram 8

THE POINT (£££)

A great location in Albert Park and stylish surroundings draw crowds, as does the seasonal modern fare.

➕ see GM map ✉ Aquatic Drive, Albert Park ☎ 9682 5544 🕐 Lunch and dinner: daily 🚋 Tram 12

SAPORE (££–£££)

This trendy restaurant serves modern Italian food in a bold, streamlined setting. Classic desserts and good value.

➕ 7L ✉ 3 Fitzroy Street, St Kilda ☎ 9534 9666
🕐 Lunch: Tue–Sun. Dinner: daily 🚋 Tram 16

SONIC (££–£££)

The modern Mediterranean dishes here are well presented, the surroundings are congenial and the prices are reasonable. Near to the MCG.

➕ 22S ✉ 80 Jolimont Street, Jolimont ☎ 9650 1807
🕐 Breakfast: Mon–Fri. Lunch and dinner: Mon–Sat.
🚋 Tram 70

STELLA (££–£££)

Food and wine come together well at this city restaurant with a menu of modern British and French dishes.

➕ 21R ✉ 159 Spring Street, Melbourne ☎ 9639 1555
🕐 Lunch: Mon–Fri. Dinner: Mon–Sat 🚋 City Circle Tram

TRYST (££–£££)

The menu of delicious dishes changes seasonally at this homely restaurant. Good service.

➕ 9J ✉ 3 Wilson Street, South Yarra ☎ 9827 5533
🕐 Lunch and dinner: daily
🚋 Tram 8, 72

'Modern Australian' cuisine

For many years Australian meals were based on the tastes of the early English settlers. Sunday dinner was nearly always roast beef or lamb and three vegetables – potatoes, pumpkin, and beans or peas; roast chicken was the big treat. Immigration brought more variety to the restaurant scene and new produce and spices. Increasing affluence enabled people to eat out more often and trained, local chefs made the expense worthwhile. Modern Australian cuisine was born, fusing food styles and ingredients from all areas of Australian society. At the same time, interest in Aboriginal foods grew, popularising bush tucker ingredients such as kangaroo, emu, crocodile and native fruits and nuts, including the now widely acclaimed macadamia nut.

EUROPEAN CUISINE

Victorian wines

Australian wines have come a long way in recent years and are now exported to Europe, the US and Asia in huge quantities. It is worth seeking out Victorian wines to go with your food, particularly those from the Yarra Valley. Varieties include Cabernet Sauvignon, Shiraz, Chardonnay and Chablis. Good winemakers to look for include De Bortoli, Best's, Yering Station and Diamond Valley.

AJAY'S (££–£££)
The owner-chef gives French cuisine a modern touch at this very popular restaurant.
🏠 7E ✉ 555 Nicholson Street, Carlton North ☎ 9380 5555
🍽 Lunch: Tue–Fri. Dinner: Tue–Sat 🚃 Tram 96

BORSATO (££)
This really excellent Italian restaurant is a bit out of the way, but the food is of a high standard and the surroundings very pleasant.
🏠 7E ✉ 450 Nicholson Street, Fitzroy North ☎ 9482 3388
🍽 Lunch: Wed–Fri. Dinner: Mon–Sat 🚃 Tram 96

CAFFE E CUCINA (££–£££)
Long popular with the glitterati and deservedly so, since the Italian food here is always delicious.
🏠 8J ✉ 581 Chapel Street, South Yarra ☎ 9827 4139
🍽 Breakfast, lunch and dinner: Mon–Sat 🚃 Tram 8

THE EUROPEAN (££–£££)
A city favourite with French and Italian dishes, perfect ambience and great service.
🏠 21Q ✉ 161 Spring Street, Melbourne ☎ 9654 0811
🍽 Breakfast, lunch and dinner: daily 🚃 City Circle Tram

FRANCE SOIR (££–£££)
Always popular, and deservedly so for the good classic French dishes and extensive and varied wine list.
🏠 8J ✉ 11 Toorak Road, South Yarra ☎ 9866 8569

🍽 Lunch and dinner: daily
🚃 Tram 8

GROSSI FLORENTINO (£££)
One of Melbourne's oldest and best restaurants with traditional European fare. Elegant and hard to beat.
🏠 20R ✉ 80 Bourke Street, Melbourne ☎ 9662 1811
🍽 Lunch: Mon–Fri. Dinner: Mon–Sat 🚃 City Circle Tram

LA MADRAGUE (££–£££)
Perhaps the best French restaurant in Melbourne, with great bistro food.
🏠 17W ✉ 171 Buckhurst Street, South Melbourne ☎ 9699 9627 🍽 Lunch and dinner: Mon–Fri 🚃 Tram 1

MARCHETTI'S LATIN (£££)
Elegant and modern, with some of the best Italian food anywhere. Consistently popular.
🏠 20Q ✉ 55 Lonsdale Street, Melbourne ☎ 9662 1985
🍽 Lunch: Sun–Fri. Dinner: daily 🚃 City Circle Tram

SCUSA MI (£££)
Overlooking the Yarra River and the city skyline, this top Italian restaurant uses only the best ingredients in its limited menu, with terrific results.
🏠 20T ✉ Mid-level, Southgate, Southbank (short walk from city centre) ☎ 9699 4111
🍽 Lunch and dinner: daily

SEAFOOD & GREEK

CAFÉ DIONYSOS (££–£££)

A traditional Greek taverna with fresh seafood prepared in the Greek style.

⊞ 20N ⊠ 139 Cardigan Street, Carlton ☎ 9347 8766 ⏱ Lunch: Mon–Fri. Dinner: Mon–Sat 🚋 Tram 1, 3, 22

HARRY'S (££)

Close to the water at Queenscliff with mostly outdoor seating. Although you can order other dishes besides seafood, don't miss the mussels in white wine. You'll need to rent a car to get here.

⊞ off GM map to south ⊠ Princes Park, Queenscliff ☎ 5258 3750 ⏱ Lunch: Fri–Sun. Dinner: Thu–Sun

MELBOURNE OYSTER BAR (£££)

Oysters are the speciality, but fish and other seafood are presented in many ways. The giant seafood platters are popular.

⊞ 18S ⊠ 209 King Street, Melbourne ☎ 9670 1881 ⏱ Dinner: Mon–Sat 🚋 City Circle Tram

NIKITA'S GREEK TAVERN (££)

Seafood is a speciality here, but there are lots of great Greek dishes, and on Saturday nights, Greek entertainment.

⊞ 25U ⊠ 258 Swan Street, Richmond ☎ 9428 9544 ⏱ Lunch: Mon–Fri. Dinner: daily 🚋 Tram 70

PIREAUS BLUES (££)

This Greek restaurant, decorated with traditional objects from the homeland, is one of the city's more popular. Reservations essential.

⊞ 22M ⊠ 310 Brunswick Street, Fitzroy ☎ 9417 0222 ⏱ Lunch: Wed–Fri and Sun. Dinner: daily 🚋 Tram 11

RUBIRA'S (£££)

Come for the quiet location, good service and the wide variety of fish and seafood dishes.

⊞ 8F ⊠ 5 Rae Street, North Fitzroy ☎ 9489 1974 ⏱ Lunch: Tue–Fri. Dinner: Thu–Sat 🚋 Tram 11

SAILS ON THE BAY (££–£££)

Fresh seafood is the speciality of this waterfront restaurant with fine views day and night.

⊞ see GM map ⊠ 15 Elwood Foreshore, Elwood ☎ 9525 6933 ⏱ Lunch and dinner: daily 🚋 Tram 16

TOOFEY'S (££)

One of the city's top seafood restaurants, this well-established place offers the freshest seafood cooked to perfection and a well-priced wine list.

⊞ 20M ⊠ 162 Elgin Street, Carlton ☎ 9347 9838 ⏱ Lunch: Tue–Fri. Dinner: Tue–Sun 🚋 Tram 1, 22

ZAMPELIS CAFÉ GRECO (££)

A smart place that serves a great range of Greek delicacies for all three courses. No reservations.

⊞ 20T ⊠ Crown Entertainment Complex, Southbank (short walk from city centre) ☎ 9686 9733 ⏱ Lunch and dinner: daily 🚋 Flinders Street

Australian seafood

It is not surprising that seafood is so popular in this bayside city. Local specialities include Melbourne rock oysters, kingfish, enormous prawns, Tasmanian scallops, smoked salmon and South Australian tuna. Northern fish such as the delicious barramundi grace menus all over town. Appropriately, many seafood restaurants have waterfront locations, where you can buy excellent fish and chips to go – St Kilda, Brighton and Williamstown are particularly good spots for alfresco eating.

THAI & VIETNAMESE

Thai and Vietnamese cuisine

Australians have turned to Thai food in a big way in the past decade and the quality of food in the best Thai restaurants in Sydney and Melbourne is equal to that anywhere outside Thailand – light and tasty, based on very fresh produce and delicate spices and herbs. Vietnamese cuisine now rivals Thai cuisine in popularity, especially in Melbourne, where many refugees settled after the war in their homeland. Pricey Vietnamese establishments with refined cuisine are proliferating.

THE GATE (£££)

This large and lively Vietnamese restaurant offers refined cuisine in an elegant setting, plus a variety of entertainment. Reserve.

26S 545 Church Street, Richmond 9428 5127 Lunch and dinner: daily Tram 78, 79

KIN KAO (££)

Thai and Vietnamese dishes are mixed and matched in unique ways at this spare, informal restaurant, with adventurous modern cuisine.

8K Pran Central, 30 Cato Street, Prahran 9510 8788 Lunch: Mon–Sat. Dinner: Tue–Sat Tram 72

LEMONGRASS (££–£££)

Some people call this Melbourne's best Thai restaurant. The food is creative and the setting restrained and elegant. Specialises in ancient royal Thai recipes.

20N 174 Lygon Street, Carlton 9347 5204 Lunch: Mon–Fri. Dinner: Wed–Sun Tram 96

MIN TAN II (£)

A huge menu of Chinese and Vietnamese dishes, with especially good seafood, make this no-frills restaurant a favourite with discerning diners.

25Q 190 Victoria Street, Richmond 9427 7131 Lunch and dinner: daily Tram 23, 42, 109

SUKHOTHAI (£)

The smart Thai surroundings, together with a great selection of traditional food, have earned this place a string of awards.

22M 234 Johnston Street, Fitzroy 9419 4040 Dinner: daily Tram 11

SWEET BASIL (££)

Modern Thai cooking keeps company with old favourites here.

8J 209 Commercial Road, South Yarra 9827 3390 Dinner: Tue–Sun Tram 72

THAILA THAI (£)

Generous portions and a no-nonsense decor draw crowds. Takeout available.

7D 82 Lygon Street, East Brunswick 9387 0659 Dinner: Wed–Sun Tram 96

THAI THANI (££)

Locals have long known this place for its great selection of authentic food, served in ersatz Thai surroundings, at reasonable prices.

22N 293 Brunswick Street, Fitzroy 9419 6463 Dinner: daily Tram 11

VIET'S QUAN (££)

Spare and modern, with little to distract you from the food, which is authentic and just about the best value in town. Reservations suggested.

8J 300 Toorak Road, South Yarra 9827 4765 Lunch and dinner: Mon–Sat Tram 8

OTHER ASIAN RESTAURANTS

CHINA BAR (£)
A contemporary, informal spot serving a huge range of Chinese and Southeast Asian noodle and rice dishes.
🕂 20R 📧 235 Russell Street, Melbourne ☎ 9639 1633
🕐 Lunch and dinner: daily
🚋 City Circle Tram

CHINE ON PARAMOUNT (£££)
A typical Chinese restaurant where you will find authentic dishes in fine style.
🕂 20R 📧 101 Little Bourke Street, Melbourne ☎ 9699 1900
🕐 Lunch: Mon –Sat. Dinner: daily 🚋 City Circle Tram

FLOWER DRUM (£££)
Melbourne's best Chinese restaurant offers Cantonese and other regional food in stylish surroundings.
🕂 20R 📧 17 Market Lane, Melbourne ☎ 9662 3655
🕐 Lunch: Mon–Sat. Dinner: daily 🚋 City Circle Tram

KABUKI (££)
The food here is Japanese, with some main courses cooked at the table and both traditional and Western seating.
🕂 8K 📧 70–72 Commercial Road, Prahran ☎ 9529 7888
🕐 Lunch: Mon–Fri. Dinner: daily 🚋 Tram 72

MASK OF CHINA (£££)
This stylish, well-established restaurant, one of Melbourne's best, specialises in the food of Guangzhou province.
🕂 20R 📧 115 Little Bourke Street, Melbourne ☎ 9662 2116 Lunch: Sun–Fri. Dinner: daily 🚋 City Circle Tram

MURASAKAI (££)
Sashimi and sushi are specialities, although you'll also find a great variety of entrées.
🕂 21S 📧 24 Russell Street, Melbourne ☎ 9654 5437
🕐 Lunch: Mon–Fri. Dinner: Mon–Sat 🚋 City Circle Tram

NEAR EAST (£££)
The dedicated staff here has created a rare balance of East and West, with a range of Southeast Asian dishes in an elegant, modern setting. The emphasis is on fresh ingredients.
🕂 19X 📧 254 Park Street, South Melbourne ☎ 9699 1900
🕐 Lunch: Mon–Fri. Dinner: daily 🚋 Tram 1

PENANG AFFAIR (£)
This Malaysian restaurant serves all the old favourites, including curries and *laksas* (a one-dish meal of rice noodles with either chicken or seafood).
🕂 22N 📧 325 Brunswick Street, Fitzroy ☎ 9419 7594
🕐 Lunch: Tue–Fri. Dinner: daily 🚋 Tram 11

THE TANDOOR (££–£££)
A pleasant option for tandoori and other tasty northern Indian dishes.
🕂 8J 📧 517 Chapel Street, South Yarra ☎ 9827 8247
🕐 Lunch: Wed–Sun. Dinner: daily 🚋 Tram 8

WARUNG AGUS (££)
A long menu of Indonesian dishes in a Balinese setting.
🕂 18P 📧 305 Victoria Street, West Melbourne ☎ 9329 1737 🕐 Dinner: Tue–Sat 🚋 Tram 16

Melbourne's Asian restaurants

Chinese restaurants were the main source of Asian cuisine in Melbourne for many years. Now the best of Chinese cuisine has achieved a truly superb level, and it is being joined by refined cuisine from Indonesia, Burma, Taiwan, Korea, Laos and other Asian countries. Most Asian restaurants are reasonably priced and many are BYO.

67

CAFÉS

Melbourne's café scene

You don't have to walk very far between coffees in inner-city Melbourne. Most cafés serve snacks, light meals and desserts, as well as many different beverages including tea and coffee.

ARRIVERDERCI AROMA

Italian-style café serving pasta and the like with good, strong coffee.

➕ 19Q ✉ 408 Queen Street, Melbourne ☎ 9606 0530
🕐 Breakfast, lunch and dinner: Mon–Sat 🚋 City Circle Tram

BLUE TRAIN CAFÉ

A really popular place with tasty pizzas cooked in wood-fired ovens, and other light fare – and waiters who enjoy their work.

➕ 20T ✉ Mid-level, Southgate Complex, Southbank (short walk from the city centre) ☎ 9696 0111 🕐 Breakfast, lunch and dinner: daily

CAFÉ VELOCE

Interestingly, this is a part of Dutton's classic car showroom. A stylish café serving great panini and pastries.

➕ 9H ✉ 525 Church Street, Richmond ☎ 9428 8839
🕐 Breakfast, lunch and dinner: Mon–Sat 🚋 Tram 78, 79

THE CONTINENTAL CAFÉ

Noisy and smoky, this classic café has a varied menu, good live music and great coffee.

➕ 8K ✉ 134 Greville Street, Prahran ☎ 9510 9030
🕐 Breakfast, lunch and dinner: daily 🚋 Tram 78, 79

THE DECK

This European-style brasserie overlooking the Yarra and the city skyline serves light meals and coffee.

➕ 20T ✉ Southgate, Southbank (short walk from city centre) ☎ 9699 9544
🕐 Lunch and dinner: daily

GREVILLE BAR

Patrons come to see and be seen – and the food is worth it.

➕ 8K ✉ 143 Greville Street, Prahran ☎ 9529 4800
🕐 Lunch and dinner: daily
🚋 Tram 78, 79

MEDUSA

This trendy spot in the heart of the legal district has a great atmosphere and features a Mediterranean menu.

➕ 19R ✉ 191 Queen Street, Melbourne ☎ 9670 7699
🕐 Breakfast, lunch and dinner: daily 🚋 City Circle Tram

RETRO CAFÉ

The name says it all. The food is good and hearty, and there are coffees for all moods.

➕ 8E ✉ 413 Brunswick Street, Fitzroy ☎ 9419 9103
🕐 Breakfast, lunch and dinner: daily 🚋 Tram 11

STELLA AT HEIDE

Have a look at the art, but don't miss this excellent café next door, with its eclectic range of finely crafted dishes.

➕ 14C ✉ Museum of Modern Art, 7 Templestowe Road, Bulleen ☎ 9852 1406
🕐 Lunch: Tue–Sun
🚉 Heidelberg station 🚌 From station, take bus 291 and alight near the mueum

VICTORY CAFÉ

Once a railway station, this Paris-inspired café serves everything from coffee and pastries to light lunches and after-theatre snacks.

➕ 7L ✉ 60 Fitzroy Street, St Kilda ☎ 9534 3727
🕐 Breakfast, lunch and dinner: daily 🚋 Tram 16

OUT-OF-TOWN RESTAURANTS

THE HEALESVILLE HOTEL (££)

The grand old dining room of this country pub has been made over, with a contemporary menu and interesting wine list.

off GM map to north ✉ 256 Maroondah Highway, Healesville ☎ 5962 4002 🕐 Lunch and dinner: daily

KENLOCK LICENSED RESTAURANT (££)

Fine international dining and an excellent wine cellar feature at this country manor-house restaurant.

off GM map to north ✉ Mt Dandenong Tourist Road, Olinda ☎ 9751 1008 🕐 Lunch: Wed–Sun. Dinner: Fri–Sat

KOAKI RESTAURANT (££)

Corio Bay views, reasonable prices, and interesting Japanese cuisine – it's no wonder that locals love this place.

off GM map to west ✉ Rippleside Park, Drumcondra ☎ 5272 1925 🕐 Dinner: Tue–Sun

NEW SAIGON RESTAURANT (£)

Order with abandon from the selection of good Thai, Vietnamese and Chinese dishes – all are reasonably priced.

off GM map to west ✉ 211 Moorabool Street, Geelong ☎ 5221 6396 🕐 Lunch: Mon–Fri. Dinner: daily

OPUS (££–£££)

Opus with great views, serves varied, well-priced modern food.

off GM map to south ✉ 145 Hotham Road, Sorrento ☎ 5984 1770 🕐 Dinner Wed–Sat (daily in summer)

OZONE HOTEL (££)

Contemporary fare is served at this famous old hotel. Excellent wine list.

off GM map to south ✉ 42 Gellibrand Street, Queenscliff ☎ 9739 0023 🕐 Lunch and dinner daily

PEPPERS DELGANY (£££)

French, Mediterranean and Asian flavours mingle at this magnificent old place with consistently good food.

off GM map to south ✉ Point Nepean Road, Portsea ☎ 5984 4000 🕐 Breakfast, lunch and dinner: daily

RANGES AT OLINDA (£)

A bar and bistro with a great variety of dishes. In winter, the open fire keeps things cosy.

off GM map to north ✉ 5 Main Street, Olinda ☎ 9751 2133 🕐 Lunch and dinner: daily

WILD OAK CAFÉ (££)

This rustic café presents a mixed menu that includes heartier fare in winter.

off GM map to north ✉ 232 Ridge Road, Mt Dandenong ☎ 9751 2033 🕐 Lunch and dinner: daily

YARRA VALLEY DAIRY (££)

In this dairy barn, fitted out as a café, you can sample fine cheeses.

off GM map to south ✉ McMeikan's Road, Yering ☎ 5258 1011 🕐 Lunch and dinner: daily

Getting there

You will need to hire a car to reach the restaurants shown on this page.

Dinner on the Yarra

What better way to experience Melbourne at night than a dinner cruise on the Yarra River. You definitely don't go for the food – it's the scenery, featuring the city skyline and docklands, that's the major draw. Operators include Melbourne River Cruises (lunches and dinners ☎ 9614 1215), Southbank Cruises (dinner ☎ 9646 5677) and City River Cruises (☎ 9650 2214).

Shopping Centres & Department Stores

Up-market shopping

Shops at the upper end of Collins Street, and in South Yarra and Toorak, sell international designer labels (see opposite). Other international shops include Fabergé, Gucci and Tiffanys at the Crown Entertainment Complex, and the Galleria Plaza shops.

For fine jewellery fashioned from Australian pearls, opals, gold or diamonds, visit one of the jewellery shops (➤ 73).

Melbourne mega malls

A trip to any of Melbourne's major suburban shopping centres provides a chance to observe the locals in their natural habitat. You'll find cinemas and restaurants, as well as free entertainment. Try the Chadstone Shopping Centre (✆ 1341 Dandenong Road, Chadstone; 🕐 Mon–Wed, 9–5:30; Thu and Fri 9–9; Sat 9–5; Sun 10–5).

AUSTRALIA ON COLLINS

Over 65 specialist shops provide the best in fashion, food and housewares.

➕ 19S ✉ 260 Collins Street ☎ 9650 4355 🚋 City Circle Tram

THE BLOCK ARCADE

Opened in 1892, this National Trust-classified arcade has an intricately tiled floor, decorative ironwork, stained-glass windows and over 30 shops on three levels.

➕ 20S ✉ 282 Collins Street ☎ 9654 5244 🚋 City Circle Tram

COLLINS 234

Totally dedicated to fashion clothing and accessories.

➕ 20S ✉ 234 Collins Street ☎ 9650 4373 🚋 City Circle Tram

COLLINS PLACE

This large, stylish and popular shopping centre in the heart of Collins Street has many specialist shops.

➕ 20S ✉ Collins Street ☎ 9655 3600 🚋 City Circle Tram

COLLINS STREET ('PARIS END')

Many exclusive boutiques selling brand names are along this elegant stretch of Collins Street, between Swanston and Spring streets.

➕ 21R ✉ Collins Street 🚋 City Circle Tram

DAVID JONES

Known to the locals as DJs, this alternative to Myer sells quality goods. Excellent food hall in the Bourke Street shop.

➕ 20R ✉ Little Bourke, Bourke and Little Collins streets ☎ 9643 2222 🚋 City Circle Tram

GALLERIA PLAZA

Interesting collection of fashion and gift shops.

➕ 19S ✉ Corner of Elizabeth and Bourke streets ☎ 9675 6416 🚋 City Circle Tram

MELBOURNE CENTRAL

This centre, covering two city blocks, houses over 160 specialist shops and the Daimaru department store. There are also cafés, restaurants and an original building, once used in the manufacture of gunshot.

➕ 19R ✉ Corner of Swanston and LaTrobe streets ☎ 9922 1100 🚋 City Circle Tram

MYER

The biggest department store in the southern hemisphere sells a wide range of fashion, designer housewares, gifts and cosmetics.

➕ 20R ✉ Lonsdale, Little Bourke and Bourke streets ☎ 9661 1111 🚋 City Circle Tram

THE ROYAL ARCADE

Australia's oldest retail arcade, the 'Royal' contains 30 shops that sell fashion and gifts, all overseen by two statues of Gog and Magog, giants from British folklore.

➕ 20S ✉ 308 Little Collins Street 🚋 City Circle Tram

SHOPPING AREAS & SUBURBS

CARLTON

Follow your nose to delicious coffee and fresh pasta on Lygon Street, Melbourne's own Little Italy. Check out the great shopping in the surrounding area.

✚ 7F ✉ Lygon Street, Carlton ⊟ Tram 1, 22

FITZROY

The way-out shops on Brunswick Street, Melbourne's liveliest street, reflect the alternative nature of the suburb. Good for fashion, books and galleries.

✚ 8G ✉ Brunswick Street, Fitzroy ⊟ Tram 11, 86

JAM FACTORY

Home to the huge Borders bookshop, a cinema complex, food outlets and many specialist shops, this former jam factory is a destination in its own right.

✚ 8J ✉ 500 Chapel Street, South Yarra ⊟ Tram 8

RICHMOND

Apart from the suburb's Greek and Vietnamese shops, Bridge Road and Swan Street offer designer seconds outlets and other shopping experiences.

✚ 9H ✉ Bridge Road and Swan Street, Richmond ⊟ Tram 48, 70, 109

ST KILDA

Melbourne's most vibrant suburb combines beachside frivolity with serious dining, great general shopping, and a Sunday arts and crafts market (► 74). Fitzroy Street and Acland Street are essential stops.

✚ 7L ✉ Fitzroy and Acland streets, St Kilda ⊟ Tram 96

SOUTHBANK

This collection of shops and restaurants with great river views lies just across the Yarra River from the city centre, between the arts complex and the Crown Entertainment Complex.

✚ 20T ✉ Southbank (short walk from city centre)

SOUTH YARRA & PRAHRAN

The stylish clothing shops and trendy restaurants of Chapel Street and Toorak Road attract those who come to see and be seen. Retro design and a gay subculture reign on Greville Street and Commercial Road.

✚ 8K ✉ Chapel Street and Toorak Road, South Yarra; Greville Street and Commercial Road, Prahran ⊟ Tram 6, 8, 72

TOORAK VILLAGE

Famous labels, famous names and exotic gifts can all be found in the shops in this tree-lined section of Toorak Road.

✚ 10J ✉ Toorak Road, between Williams and Orrong roads, Toorak ⊟ Tram 8

WILLIAMSTOWN

A waterfront village full of art, crafts, antique shops and coffee shops. People flock here on weekends.

✚ 3K ✉ The Strand, Williamstown ⊞ Williamstown

Shopping hours

Shops in the city and in designated shopping areas are generally open 10–6 on Monday, Tuesday, Wednesday and Thursday; 10–9 on Friday; and 10–6 on Saturday and Sunday. Individual shop hours do vary, so call ahead, especially at weekends.

Shopping tours

To explore out-of-the-way bargain shopping districts, you might want to call one of the following operators, which organise guided shopping tours. Shopping Spree Tours (☎ 9596 6600) specialises in warehouse shopping for clothing and other goods at wholesale prices, and packages personalised and upmarket tours. The Melbourne Ambassadors Specialist Shopping Tour (☎ 99639 4044) is personalised, but pricey.

AUSTRALIANA

Local crafts and souvenirs

Original Australian design tends to be influenced by nature. Natural materials such as indigenous timbers are used to produce decorative sculptural objects and utilitarian pieces, and wool is often crafted into what could be best described as 'wearable art'. Silver and gold jewellery featuring Australian floral motifs is particularly popular with visitors.

Shop at the National Wool Museum

An excellent range of wool products is for sale at Australia's only comprehensive wool museum, housed in a century-old wool store and featuring displays and hands-on exhibits highlighting all facets of this industry.

off GM map to east ✉ 16 Moorabool Street, Geelong ☎ 5227 0701 ⊙ Daily 9–5

ABORIGINAL CREATIONS
Indigenous Australian designs in fine clothing, textiles, accessories and artefacts.
21R ✉ 50 Bourke Street ☎ 9662 9400 🚉 Parliament

ABORIGINAL HANDCRAFTS
The sale of handcrafts through this non-profit organisation has supported communities since the 1970s.
20R ✉ 9/125 Swanston Street ☎ 9650 4717 🚉 Flinders Street

AUSTRALIAN WAY
Australian clothing, Aboriginal art, souvenirs and gifts.
20S ✉ 260 Collins Street ☎ 9654 3021 🚋 City Circle Tram

BODY MAP AUSTRALIA
Australian clothes and more unusual souvenirs including eucalyptus leaf embossed table mats and leather hats.
19R ✉ Melbourne Central ☎ 9428 4577 🚋 City Circle Tram

CUSTOMS WHARF GALLERY
Australian art, crafts, sculpture, glass, textiles, jewellery and housewares are sold in a beautifully restored old building in the heart of historic Williamstown.
3K ✉ 126 Nelson Place, Williamstown ☎ 9399 9726 ⛴ Williamstown ferry

EUGENE AUSTRALIA
Renowned for elegant fashions, furs, souvenirs

and accessories inspired by the outback.
20S ✉ 161 Collins Street ☎ 9650 5611 🚋 City Circle Tram

KEN DUNCAN GALLERY
Outstanding images of Australian landscapes by one of the world's leading exponents of panoramic photography.
20T ✉ Shop U6, Southgate (short walk from city centre) ☎ 9686 8022

KIRRA
Fine Australian gifts, sculpture and decorative arts designed and handcrafted in Australia.
20T ✉ Shop M7, Southgate (short walk from city centre) ☎ 9682 7923

KOORI CONNECTIONS 'ALTAIR'
Authentic Aboriginal arts and crafts gallery owned and operated by Aboriginal people.
19P ✉ 155 Victoria Street, Melbourne ☎ 9326 9824 🚋 City Circle Tram

MATCHBOX
One of Melbourne's longest established gift shops, specialising in design and new concepts and trends.
9K ✉ 1050 High Street, Armadale ☎ 9500 0311 🚋 Tram 6

R M WILLIAMS
Authentic Australian outback clothing and traditional Aussie footwear.
19R ✉ Melbourne Central, 300 Lonsdale Street ☎ 9663 7126 🚋 City Circle Tram

JEWELLERY & GEMSTONES

ABBESS OPAL MINE
Good opal stones and jewellery, as well as coin watches, Australian pearls, woollen wear and kangaroo and sheepskin products.

✚ 20R ✉ 218–220 Swanston Street ☎ 9639 2188 ▣ City Circle Tram

ASHLEY OPALS JEWELERS
Fine opals, opal jewellery, Australian South Sea pearls and Argyle diamonds.

✚ 21R ✉ 85 Collins Street ☎ 9654 4866 ▣ City Circle Tram

BODY ART
Lovely original design jewellery.

✚ 19R ✉ Melbourne Central ☎ 9429 8247 ▣ City Circle Tram

CODY OPAL
A leading supplier to the international jewellery industry, plus a museum displaying fossilised opals.

✚ 20R ✉ 119 Swanston Street ☎ 9654 5533 ▣ City Circle Tram

DESERT GEMS
Handmade jewellery from top Australian craftspeople.

✚ 20T ✉ Shop U9, Southgate (short walk from city centre) ☎ 9696 8211

ELIZABETH'S
Worth seeking out for its unique range of Melbourne-made jewellery in gold, silver and gemstones.

✚ 20T ✉ Shop M2, Southgate (short walk from city centre) ☎ 9696 7944

GEMTEC
Manufactures and sells jewellery set with opals.

✚ 20S ✉ 243 Collins Street ☎ 9654 5733 ▣ City Circle Tram

JOHNSTON OPALS
One of Melbourne's oldest opal dealers stocks a large selection of opals and Australian souvenirs.

✚ 21R ✉ 124 Exhibition Street ☎ 9650 7434 ▣ City Circle Tram

KAISERMAN
Individually designed pieces, plus top brand-name watches, since 1926.

✚ 8J ✉ 586 Chapel Street, South Yarra ☎ 9824 1088 ▣ Tram 78, 79

MAKERS MARK
Representing Australia's finest studio jewellers and craftspeople, with designs made from South Sea pearls and Argyle diamonds.

✚ 21R ✉ 101 Collins Street ☎ 9826 2411 ▣ City Circle Tram

J H MULES OPALS
Opals at this store, in operation since 1922, come from its three mines in the Lightning Ridge opal fields.

✚ 21R ✉ 110 Exhibition Street ☎ 99650 3566 ▣ City Circle Tram

RUTHERFORD ANTIQUES
Purveys a superb range of fine sterling silver and antique jewellery from Georgian to art deco.

✚ 20S ✉ 186 Collins Street ☎ 9650 7878 ▣ City Circle Tram

Australian gems and jewellery

Opals are the most popular gemstones sought out by visitors although you'll also find South Sea pearls, Argyle diamonds and original designs in Australian gold. Visit several shops to get an idea of the variety and price range before deciding on your purchase. Many shops have examples of rough stones and a few even have displays explaining the mining process. All are happy to answer questions.

MARKETS

Bargain shopping

The post-Christmas season, from late December into January, is bargain shopping time. So is mid-winter, in June and July. You can shop for clothing on a budget at any time in department and chain stores. Head to Richmond, where shops selling designer seconds and other well-priced clothes are plentiful. Inner city suburbs offer bargains in second-hand clothing and many other items.

ARMADALE ANTIQUES CENTRE

Forty dealers sell a range of quality antiques and collectibles in this centre at the heart of High Street's antique area.

➕ 10K ✉ 1147 High Street, Armadale ☎ 9822 7788 🕙 Daily 9–5 🚋 Tram 6

CAMBERWELL SUNDAY MARKET

Several hundred stallholders converge here to sell assorted trash and treasures. A great place to observe the slow drift of suburban life.

➕ 12H ✉ Station Street, Camberwell 🕙 Sun 9–5 🚋 Tram 70

GREVILLE STREET SUNDAY MARKET

Appropriately sited on a hip and trendy street, this market sells retro goods and many things alternative.

➕ 8K ✉ Greville Street, Prahran 🕙 Sun 12–5 🚋 Tram 78, 79

PIPEWORKS FUN MARKET

The 500 shops, covered stalls, and two food courts of this unique market complex sprawl over 8 hectares. Live entertainment. You'll need a taxi to get here.

➕ see GM map ✉ 400 Mahoneys Street, Campbellfield 🕙 Sat and Sun 9–5

PRAHRAN MARKET

This lively favourite, a short walk from Chapel Street, sells fresh produce and delicatessen goods.

➕ 8K ✉ 163–185 Commercial Road 🕙 Tue and Thu 10–5; Fri 6–6; Sat 6–1 🚋 Tram 8, 72 to Chapel Street

QUEEN VICTORIA MARKET

On Sundays, Melbourne's most popular and varied food market also sells clothing, gift items, accessories and housewares.

➕ 19Q ✉ Corner of Elizabeth and Victoria streets, Melbourne ☎ 9320 5822 🕙 Tue and Thu 6–2; Fri 6–6; Sat 6–3; Sun 9–4 🚋 City Circle Tram

SOUTH MELBOURNE

The stallholders at this market sell everything from fresh fruit and vegetables to delicatessen items and household goods.

➕ 18N ✉ Corner of Cecil and York streets ☎ 9209 6295 🕙 Wed 8–2; Fri 8–6; Sat and Sun 8–4 🚋 South Melbourne

ST KILDA ESPLANADE MARKET

Original works made by stallholders at this popular Sunday arts and crafts market draw shoppers from far and wide.

➕ 7L ✉ The Esplanade, St Kilda 🕙 Sun 10–4 🚋 Tram 15, 16, 96

THE SUNDAY ART MARKET

An essential stop for interesting and unusual handcrafted works in the cultural hub of Melbourne.

➕ 21T ✉ Victorian Arts Centre 🕙 Sun 10–6 🚋 Flinders Street

BOOKS

ANGUS & ROBERTSON BOOKWORLD

A good general selection of current titles plus several bins of discounted books.

🞠 20S ✉ 35 Swanston Street ☎ 9650 3652 🚋 City Circle Tram

BORDERS

Melbourne's largest and most comprehensive book stockists with a very large range of travel publications.

🞠 8J ✉ 500 Chapel Street, South Yarra ☎ 9824 2299 🚋 Trams 78, 79

BRUNSWICK STREET BOOKSTORE

This excellent, eclectic shop has all the latest titles and more, plus plenty of places to sit and read.

🞠 8J ✉ 305 Brunswick Street, Fitzroy ☎ 9416 1030 🚋 Tram 11

COLLINS

New books plus a good general backlist selection, and many discounted recent titles.

🞠 19R ✉ 104 Elizabeth Street ☎ 9650 9755 🚋 City Circle Tram

DYMOCKS

A range of new releases, a good backlist, and many books on Melbourne.

🞠 21R ✉ Shop 31/32 Collins Place ☎ 9650 9755 🚋 City Circle Tram

HILL OF CONTENT

Solid in current titles, with some specials and an excellent selection of cookbooks.

🞠 21R ✉ 86 Bourke Street ☎ 9654 2755 🚋 City Circle Tram

THE HAUNTED BOOKSHOP

More than a bookstore; there's an amazing collection of paraphernalia and books relating to spiritualism, witchcraft and medieval subjects.

🞠 19S ✉ 15 McKillop Street ☎ 9670 2585 🚋 City Circle Tram

KAY CRADDOCK

One of Melbourne's top secondhand and rare books dealers.

🞠 21R ✉ 156 Collins Street ☎ 9654 8506 🕐 Mon–Sat 9–5 🚋 City Circle Tram

MARY MARTIN BOOKSHOP

This stylish shop is a delightful place to browse. There's an excellent Australiana section.

🞠 20T ✉ Shop G18, Southgate, Southbank (short walk from city centre) ☎ 9332 4581 🕐 Daily 9–5

McGILLS

One of the largest technical bookshops in Australia, a good source for elusive titles.

🞠 19R ✉ 187 Elizabeth Street ☎ 9602 5566 🚋 City Circle Tram

READINGS

One of Melbourne's top bookshops, which sells an excellent range of the latest titles and CDs.

🞠 20N ✉ 309 Lygon Street, Carlton ☎ 9650 9755 🚋 Tram 1, 22

Books on Australia

Photographic books documenting contemporary Melbourne make good souvenirs, and there are many. To find out what the city was like in the 19th century, read *The Rise and Fall of Marvellous Melbourne* by Graeme Davidson.

To learn about the original inhabitants, read *Aboriginal Australians* by Richard Broome.

Tim Flannery's *The Future Eaters* is a fascinating ecological history of Australia.

FOOD & WINE

Australian delicacies

To get an idea of the best Australian produce, be sure to visit the Queen Victoria Market (► 74), where stall holders allow you to sample cheeses, meats and exotic fruits. Look for cheese from the Yarra Valley and Tasmania, and seafood from the cooler southern oceans – everything from scallops to Tasmanian smoked salmon (specialist fishmongers will cook your selection). Fruits grown in Victoria include strawberries, pears and apples. Vegetables such as snow peas, asparagus and broccoli are plentiful, as well as the only native nut to hit the world stage, the macadamia.

A1 MIDDLE EASTERN FOOD STORE

All the hard-to-get spices, oils and other exotic ingredients are here, plus breads and sweets.

➕ 7C ✉ 43 Sydney Road, Brunswick ☎ 9386 04406 🚋 Tram 19

DAVID JONES FOOD HALL

The lower level of this food hall is one of the city's most exclusive food shops. The great variety of produce includes Australian wines, beers, cheeses, meats, seafood, fruit and vegetables.

➕ 20R ✉ 299 Bourke Street ☎ 9643 2222 🚋 City Circle Tram

DE BORTOLI WINERY AND RESTAURANT

One of the best restaurants in the Yarra Valley, with fantastic views. The northern Italian food served here is mostly based on local produce and comes with a choice of the vineyard vintages. Car needed.

➕ off GM map to north ✉ Pinnacle Lane, Dixons Creek ☎ 5965 2271

JIMMY WATSON'S WINE BAR

This Melbourne institution is the place to socialise and sample wines of great quality. Check out the cellar.

➕ 20M ✉ 333 Lygon Street, Carlton ☎ 9347 3985 🚋 Tram 96

MELBOURNE WINE ROOM

Sampling the many Victorian wines at the old bar can precede a Mediterranean-inspired meal.

➕ 7L ✉ The George Hotel, 125 Fitzroy Street, St Kilda ☎ 9525 5599 🚋 Tram 16

PHILLIPPA'S BAKERY & PROVISIONS STORE

There's not much room to eat in here, but the huge selection of breads, cakes and other produce can yield a tasty take-away lunch or picnic.

➕ 10K ✉ 1030 High Street, Armadale ☎ 9576 2020 🚋 Tram 6

RATHDOWNE STREET FOOD STORE

All sorts of well-prepared dishes from pasta to curries are available to take away.

➕ 7E ✉ 617 Rathdowne Street, Carlton North ☎ 9347 4064 🚋 Tram 96

RICHMOND HILL CAFÉ AND LARDER

Food expert Stephanie Alexander's fine condiments and fresh produce are for sale here as well as a huge selection of cheeses. The place doubles as a café serving tasty, fresh meals.

➕ 8H ✉ 48 Bridge Road, Richmond ☎ 9421 2808 🚋 Tram 75

WALTER'S WINE AND FOOD STORE

Choose from hundreds of Australian wines, including older vintages, and a great array of food to eat in or take away.

➕ 20T ✉ Shop U1/2, Southgate, Southbank (short walk from city centre) ☎ 9690 3200

SPECIALIST SHOPS

ABC SHOP
Operated by the Australian Broadcasting Corporation, this interesting shop offers books, videos, music and audio cassettes, CDs, toys and clothes relating to Australian TV and radio programmes.

✚ 19R ✉ Corner of Elizabeth and Bourke streets ☎ 9626 1167 🚊 City Circle Tram

ARTS CENTRE SHOP
Offers an excellent selection of arts-related merchandise, showcasing works by artists and craftspeople along with inexpensive gifts.

✚ 20T ✉ 100 St Kilda Road ☎ 9281 8285 🚊 Tram 3, 5

AUSTRALIAN GEOGRAPHIC SHOP
Australia's best artists, writers, photographers, craftspeople and designers join forces to produce clothing, prints, stationary, bird houses, telescopes and more.

✚ 19R ✉ Level 1, Melbourne Central ☎ 9639 2478 🚊 City Circle Tram

CITY HATTERS
An Akubra hat from this shop provides good protection from the harsh Aussie sun.

✚ 20S ✉ 211 Flinders Street ☎ 9614 3294 🚊 City Circle Tram

COUNTRY ROAD
An Australian success story, with shops abroad as well as in Melbourne Central, Carlton, South Yarra and Brighton, Country Road specialises in casual clothes for men and women, and home furnishings.

✚ 19R ✉ Melbourne Central ☎ 9663 1766 🚊 City Circle Tram

EN ROUTE
The city's leading specialist shop for luggage stocks briefcases, handbags, wallets and backpacks.

✚ 8J ✉ 280 Toorak Road, South Yarra ☎ 9827 4709 🚊 Tram 8

GASLIGHT MUSIC
One of Melbourne's finest tape and CD shops, with a particularly good selection of Australian music. Sells everything from classical music to comedy.

✚ 21R ✉ 85 Bourke Street ☎ 9650 9009 🚊 City Circle Tram

MELBOURNE SURF SHOP
Everything for the surfer, from boards to beachwear, including the popular Billabong, Rip Curl and Hot Tuna brands. Well worth visiting.

✚ 20R ✉ Tivoli Arcade, 249 Bourke Street ☎ 9654 8403 🚊 City Circle Tram

SPORTS CAPITAL
This unique showcase for major sporting events in Melbourne (and Australia) sells good sports equipment and clothing for men and women.

✚ 19R ✉ Shop 206, Melbourne Central, La Trobe Street ☎ 9663 7122 🚊 City Circle Tram

Passionate about shopping
Meburnians have a great love of shopping and this has certainly rubbed off on the visitors; it is a highlight for many coming to the city. The hot spots (➤ 70–71) are easy to find, but also get on the tram and visit the suburbs to find some specialist and individual shops.

THEATRE & CLASSICAL MUSIC

The cinema scene

Melbourne's cinema scene is thriving. Of the many cinemas, the main complexes are on Bourke and Russell streets and at the Jam Factory and at the Crown Entertainment Complex. More alternative cinemas include the Longford in South Yarra, the Kino at Collins Place and the Capital Theatre at 113 Swanston Street. For foreign and offbeat films try the Lumiere at 108 Lonsdale Street. Schedules are in the *Age* and the *Herald Sun*.

Classical Melbourne

The Victorian Arts Centre offers excellent opera, ballet and classical music. The world-renowned Melbourne Symphony Orchestra, the Australian Ballet and Australian opera companies all perform here regularly. The Melbourne Theatre Company has a regular season of productions at the State Theatre, while the complex's Playhouse presents a variety of theatrical productions. Classical music concerts are also given at the Town Hall and the Conservatorium of Music.

COMEDY THEATRE

This delightful small theatre, modeled on a Florentine palace, with a Spanish-style interior, hosts a variety of shows.
✚ 21R ✉ 240 Exhibition Street ☎ 9209 9000 🚋 City Circle Tram

FORUM

Originally a picture palace, the Forum retains its dramatic interior but now hosts concerts and other events.
✚ 21S ✉ Corner of Flinders and Russell streets ☎ 9299 9864 🚋 City Circle Tram

HER MAJESTY'S THEATRE

This lovely old theatre, built in 1866, is one of Melbourne's leading locations for musicals and other major theatrical productions.
✚ 21R ✉ 219 Exhibition Street ☎ 9663 3211 🚋 City Circle Tram

LA MAMA THEATRE

One of the city's principal venues for new theatre showcases Australian talent.
✚ 20N ✉ 205 Faraday Street, Carlton ☎ 9347 6142 🚋 Tram 96

MELBOURNE CONCERT HALL

This is the city's prime performing arts venue. Look for performances by Melbourne Opera Company, Melbourne Symphony Orchestra, and Australian Ballet.
✚ 20T ✉ Victorian Arts Centre, Southbank ☎ 9281 8000 🎧 call for hall tours 🚋 Flinders Street 🚋 Tram 3, 5, 6, 8

MELBOURNE TOWN HALL

A major site of choral and orchestral performances, with occasional free Sunday concerts.
✚ 20R ✉ Swanston Street ☎ 9658 9658 🚋 City Circle Tram

PRINCESS THEATRE

Melbourne's most glorious performance space, in one of the city's finest buildings, is home to musicals and other leading theatrical events.
✚ 21Q ✉ 163 Spring Street ☎ 9299 9861 🚋 City Circle Tram

THE REGENT THEATRE

Opened in 1929 as a picture palace, the Regent is now equipped for both stage and screen and includes the dramatic Spanish rococo Plaza Ballroom.
✚ 21R ✉ 191 Collins Street ☎ 9299 9864 🚋 City Circle Tram

STATE THEATRE

The home of the excellent Melbourne Theatre Company, this intimate theatre also hosts Melbourne Dance Company performances.
✚ 20T ✉ Victorian Arts Centre, Southbank ☎ 9281 8000 🕐 Shows: Mon–Sat 🚋 Flinders Street 🚋 Tram 3, 5, 6, 8

THEATREWORKS

Alternative and experimental community theatre.
✚ 7L ✉ 14 Acland Street, St Kilda ☎ 9534 4879 🚋 Tram 16

MODERN LIVE MUSIC

BENNETTS LANE JAZZ CLUB

One of the best in Melbourne, this small jazz venue attracts top names playing a variety of jazz styles.

✚ 20Q ✉ 25 Bennetts Lane ☎ 9663 2856 ⏰ Nightly 🚋 City Circle Tram

CONTINENTAL

Downstairs is a café, while upstairs musicians perform anything from rock, jazz and blues to country on most nights.

✚ 8K ✉ 134 Greville Street, Prahran ☎ 9510 2788 ⏰ Nightly 🚋 Tram 78, 79

CORNER HOTEL

Listen to a great range of cutting-edge music at this Melbourne institution with a changing line-up of bands.

✚ 8H ✉ 57 Swan Street, Richmond ☎ 9427 7300 ⏰ Most nights 🚋 Tram 70

THE ESPLANADE

On weekends, local music lovers pack this St Kilda institution, a legend among those who love pub music. You can have a meal in the restaurant at the back or watch the sunset.

✚ 7L ✉ Upper Esplanade, St Kilda ☎ 9534 0211 ⏰ Daily 🚋 Tram 16

THE KITTEN CLUB

Yellow leather chairs and pouffes, a long bar with stools and varied live music some nights. Stylish venue.

✚ 20R ✉ 2/267 Little Collins Street ☎ 9650 2448 ⏰ Tue–Sun 4PM–3AM 🚋 City Circle Tram

MELBOURNE ENTERTAINMENT CENTRE

Everything from concerts by touring international rock groups to indoor sports matches fill Melbourne's largest entertainment establishment.

✚ 8H ✉ Swan Street ☎ 9286 1600 🚋 Tram 70

PALAIS THEATRE

Built as a cinema in the 1920s, this St Kilda landmark presents live performances and shows.

✚ 7L ✉ The Esplanade, St Kilda ☎ 9534 0651 ⏰ Most nights 🚋 Tram 16

P J O'BRIENS

A boisterous and somewhat beery alternative to the standard high-tech venue, this place has standard faux Irish decor with live Irish music.

✚ 20T ✉ Southgate Complex, (short walk from city centre) ☎ 9686 5011 ⏰ Nightly

THE PURPLE EMERALD

Groovy and retro, with live jazz and blues.

✚ 20S ✉ 191 Flinders Lane ☎ 9650 7753 ⏰ Nightly, Wed–Sun 🚋 City Circle Tram

RAINBOW HOTEL

Cold beer and great bands are the primary attraction at this popular hotel.

✚ 22N ✉ 27 St David Street, Fitzroy ☎ 9525 3599 ⏰ Daily 🚋 Tram 11

Buying a ticket

There are several ways of obtaining tickets for theatre, live music concerts and other events. You can visit the box offices, or purchase by credit card from ticketing agencies such as Ticketmaster (☎ 136 166) and Ticketek (☎ 132 849). At Half Tix (☎ 1900 939 436), a booth in Bourke Street Mall, you can get discounted tickets on the day of performance. At the latter, tickets must be bought in person and you must pay in cash Mon 10–2; Tue–Fri 11–6; Sat 10–2.

HOTELS & BARS

Melbourne's watering holes

When white settlers first established towns in Australia, the pub was often the first substantial building to be erected. Today there are are countless pubs and bars. The most popular local brew in Melbourne is Fosters, closely followed by Victoria Bitter (VB). Try the more unusual brews such as Hahn and Coopers, and Bundaberg rum (Bundy), made from Queensland sugar cane—the only indigenous spirit. Hotels are generally open until 11PM. Nightclubs and discos usually stay open longer.

BRIDIE O'REILLY'S

This popular Irish hotel serves all the favourites from the old country, plus good music, typical Irish decor and furnishings, and friendly company.

➕ 8J ✉ 462 Chapel Street, South Yarra ☎ 9827 7788 🕐 Mon—Wed 11—1am; Thu—Sat 11—3am 🚊 Tram 78, 79

DAN O'CONNELL HOTEL

A warm and welcoming Irish atmosphere and live music seven days a week.

➕ 21N ✉ 225 Canning Street, Carlton ☎ 9347 1502 🕐 Daily 🚊 Tram 96

DIVA BAR

Gay pub with a wide selection of music, from stage shows to current releases. Occasional dancing on the bar.

➕ 8K ✉ 153 Commercial Road, South Yarra ☎ 9826 5500 🕐 2—1am 🚊 Tram 78, 79

DOG'S BAR

When you've finished with the serious Acland Street shopping, try this bar for great antipasto and canapés.

➕ 7L ✉ 54 Acland Street, St Kilda ☎ 9525 3599 🕐 Daily 🚊 Tram 16

FIDEL'S CIGAR LOUNGE

Looking for that favourite cigar? Fidel's is sure to have it, plus drinks and lots of smoke.

➕ 20T ✉ Crown Entertainment Complex, Southbank ☎ 9292 6885 🕐 Daily 🚊 Flinders Street Tram 10, 12, 96, 109

GIN PALACE

Where serious drinkers come for the classic martinis and the stylish ambience.

➕ 20R ✉ 190 Little Collins Street (enter from Russell Place) ☎ 9654 0533 🕐 Daily 🚊 City Circle Tram

PRINCE OF WALES

The rest of the building, now spruced up, houses the excellent Circa restaurant, but the main bar is the same old popular watering hole for the locals.

➕ 7L ✉ 29 Fitzroy Street, St Kilda ☎ 9534 0011 🕐 Daily 🚊 Tram 16

THE PROVINCIAL HOTEL

One of Brunswick Street's most popular haunts serves great food, and a huge open fire keeps everyone warm in winter.

➕ 22M ✉ 299 Brunswick Street, Fitzroy ☎ 9417 2228 🕐 Daily 🚊 Tram 11

SAVI BAR & CAFÉ

Very stylish, with views of the city skyline, this popular destination serves tasty food and a full range of drinks.

➕ 20T ✉ Mid-level, Southgate ☎ 9699 3600 🕐 Daily till late

YOUNG AND JACKSON'S

The city's most famous pub and the location of the stunning nude *Chloe*, a painting that shocked the city in the late 19th century.

➕ 20S ✉ 1 Swanston Street ☎ 9650 3884 🕐 Daily 🚊 City Circle Tram

NIGHTLIFE

BAR CODE
This round the clock operation with the techno thumping away in the background is a popular spot. Has the latest video games.

✚ 19T ✉ Crown Entertainment Complex, Southbank (short walk from city centre) ☎ 9292 8888 🕐 Nightly from 8PM

BARRACUDA
One of Melbourne's most popular dance venues. The cocktail bar here is a crowd puller.

✚ 23P ✉ 64 Smith Street, Fitzroy ☎ 9417 2869 🕐 Mon–Fri 11:30–midnight; Sat 12–1AM 🚋 Tram 98

CHASERS
The latest dance music, old favourites and requests.

✚ 8J ✉ 386 Chapel Street, South Yarra ☎ 9827 6615 🕐 Nightly 🚋 Trams 78, 79

CLUB ODEON
Melbourne's live music home with the city's top DJs spinning tunes from the 1970s, 80s and 90s.

✚ 19T ✉ Level 3, Crown Entertainment Complex, Southbank ☎ 9682 1888 🕐 Nightly from 9PM

THE DOME
Progressive and vocal house music to dance to; locals really love this place.

✚ 8J ✉ 19 Commercial Road, South Yarra ☎ 9529 8966 🕐 Fri–Sat 🚋 Tram 72

HEAT
A cool spot with a cocktail lounge and club, and varied entertainment.

✚ 19T ✉ Crown Entertainment Complex, Southbank ☎ 9699 2222 🕐 Nightly

MERCURY LOUNGE
Great acoustics and live pub-style bands most nights. DJs keep the show moving and the small dance floor busy.

✚ 19T ✉ Crown Entertainment Complex, Southbank ☎ 9292 5480 🕐 Nightly from 8PM

THE METRO
Contemporary architecture, computer-based lighting and advanced audio-video technology make this one of Melbourne's great night spots.

✚ 20T ✉ Crown Entertainment Complex, Southbank ☎ 9663 4288 🕐 Nightly from 8PM

THE NIGHT CAT
This popular 1950s place spins rock 'n' roll on Wednesdays and cool jazz from Thursday to Sunday.

✚ 23N ✉ 141 Johnson Street, Fitzroy ☎ 9417 0090 🕐 Wed–Sun 8–1 🚋 Tram 11

SARATOGA
A small dance club with progressive house music and a bar atmosphere. A favourite haunt of entertainers.

✚ 21R ✉ 46 Albert Road, South Melbourne ☎ 9699 8177 🕐 Until 7AM 🚋 Tram 12

THREE FACES
This club plays mainly, but not exclusively, vocal house and commercial dance music, and presents drag shows.

✚ 8J ✉ 143 Commercial Road, South Yarra ☎ 9826 0933 🕐 Thu–Sat 🚋 Tram 72

Getting home
Trams stop running at midnight from Monday to Saturday and at 11PM on Sundays. You can use the Nightrider bus service that operates between 12:30am and 4:30am on Saturdays and Sundays (➤ 91). Alternatively take a taxi (➤ 91).

Gay and lesbian Melbourne
Melbourne has a vibrant gay and lesbian scene, especially in the area around Commercial Road in South Yarra. Many hotels, bars and clubs here cater to both gays and lesbians. Popular venues include the Diva Bar (➤ 80), the Exchange Hotel (✉ 119 Commercial Road, South Yarra), and the Glasshouse Hotel (✉ 51 Gipps Street, Collingwood).

For information on what's happening, pick up a copy of *Melbourne Star Observer* or *Brother Sister*.

SPORT

Watersports

Melbourne's location on Port Phillip Bay provides great opportunities for water sports. You can surf at Mornington Peninsula and near Flinders (► 51), windsurf from Sandringham (☎ 9598 2867), go diving in the bay (☎ 9459 4111), or sail with the Melbourne Sailing School (☎ 9589 1433). Swim at the bayside beaches close to Melbourne, between Port Melbourne and St Kilda, and from St Kilda to Portsea, and in the many public swimming pools around the city and in the suburbs.

ACTION ADVENTURES
Try your hand at abseiling, take a challenging mountain-bike ride and finish with a tranquil canoe tour in the spectacular Grampians National Park.
✉ PO Box 81, Halls Gap
☎ 5356 4540 ⏰ Daily tours

ALBERT PARK PUBLIC GOLF COURSE
This easily accessible complex offers an 18-hole course, an 18-hole putting green and other facilities all for very reasonable rates.
✚ 7K ✉ Queens Road, Albert Park ☎ 9510 5588 ⏰ Daily 6–10 🚃 Tram 16

BALLOON SUNRISE
An adventurous way to view Melbourne is to take a hot-air balloon flight followed by a champagne breakfast.
✚ 24U ✉ 41 Dover Street, Richmond ☎ 9427 7596
⏰ Daily at sunrise

BASKETBALL
Melbourne Park is the home of the NBL basketball teams, the Melbourne Tigers and the Melbourne Titans, who compete in the national competitions.
✚ 22U ✉ Melbourne Park ☎ 9576 2427 ⏰ Oct–Apr: usually Fri, Sat 🚃 Tram 70

CITY BATHS
This historic swimming complex is the place to get in a few laps or to just cool off on a hot day. Also has a gym, jacuzzis, saunas and squash courts.
✚ 20Q ✉ 420 Swanston Street ☎ 9663 5888
⏰ Mon–Fri 6AM–10PM, Sat–Sun 8–6 🚃 Swanston Street Tram

CLIFFHANGER CLIMBING GYM
Australia's tallest and most sophisticated indoor rock climbing facility; walls range from 6m to 20m tall.
✚ off GM map to east
✉ Grieve Parade, Altona North
☎ 9369 6400 ⏰ Daily

COLONIAL STADIUM
This new super-stadium was designed for a variety of sports, including Australian Rules football and cricket, as well as concerts.
✚ 17S ✉ Docklands, Melbourne ☎ 9651 6777
⏰ Call for details 🚃 City Circle Tram

DINNER PLAIN TRAIL RIDES
Based in the Dinner Plain Valley, near Mt Hotham, this company offers one day and multi-day riding trips into remote alpine areas.
✉ PO Box 31, Dinner Plain
☎ 5159 6445 🚃 Rides on demand

FITZROY SWIMMING POOL
Escape the hot streets of the city with a cool off in the main or kids' pool.
✚ 4F ✉ Alexandra Parade
☎ 9417 6493 ⏰ Daily all year 🚃 Tram 11

FLEMINGTON RACECOURSE
This famous racecourse hosts the annual Melbourne Cup and has a regular programme of race days year-round.

🚻 4F ✉ Smithfield Road, Flemington ☎ 9371 7171 🚋 Tram 57

GREAT OCEAN ROAD GOLF TOURS

This fully escorted and inclusive golf tour takes you along the Great Ocean Road. A diverse range of courses are played, including the unique Anglesea course where kangaroos are a feature.

🚻 off GM map to south ✉ 35 Hobson Street, Queenscliff ☎ 5258 3070 🕐 Tours on demand

KAYAK ADVENTURES

Explore the sea at close quarters along Victoria's spectacular coast: Wilsons Promontory, Cape Otway, the Twelve Apostles and more.

🚻 see GM map ✉ 12 Clonard Avenue, Elsternwick ☎ 9596 8876 🕐 Tours on demand

MELBOURNE CRICKET GROUND

The legendary MCG hosts cricket matches in summer. Winter is for soccer and Australian Rules football.

🚻 23T ✉ Jolimont Road ☎ 9657 8879 🕐 Tours: daily 🚋 Tram 48, 75

MELBOURNE PARK

There is no better place to watch tennis than this stadium, home to the Australian Open in January.

🚻 22U ✉ Batman Avenue ☎ 9286 1600 🕐 Call for details 🚋 Tram 70

MOONRAKER DOLPHIN SWIMS

On boat tours in pristine Port Phillip Bay, you may choose to swim with the wild dolphins or simply sightsee in comfort.

🚻 off GM map to south ✉ St Aubins Way, Sorrento ☎ 5984 4211 🕐 Tours on demand

MELBOURNE SPORTS AND AQUATIC CENTRE

There are a variety of swimming pools here as well as a popular wave pool. Other sports include table tennis, basketball, squash and volleyball.

🚻 7J ✉ Albert Park Road, Albert Park ☎ 9926 1555 🕐 Mon–Fri 9AM–10PM; Sat, Sun 8AM–8PM 🚋 Tram 12

RACING VICTORIA

Meet the locals, have a delicious meal, and watch thoroughbreds racing at one of the many metropolitan and county racetracks.

🚻 4E ✉ 400 Epsom Road, Flemington ☎ 9258 4763 🕐 Call for details 🚋 Tram 57

ROYAL PARK

The perfect venue for walking, cycling, tennis, roller-blading and jogging. There are also facilities for golf, football and cricket (➤ 45).

🚻 6F ✉ Off Royal Parade, Parkville ☎ 9568 8713 🕐 Daily during daylight hours 🚋 Tram 19

RIVIERA NAUTIC

Sail to a variety of destinations on a choice of yachts with all equipment provided.

🚻 off GM map to south ✉ Chinamans Creek, Metung ☎ 5156 2243 🕐 On demand

Crown Casino

The largest casino outside the United States, the Crown Casino at Southbank, a short walk from the city centre, is part of the Crown Entertainment Complex, which also includes a 500-room hotel. The main gaming area has 350 tables offering pontoon, roulette, baccarat, craps, *sic bo*, *pai gow* and Australia's own favourite, two-up. There are 2,500 gaming machines as well as live entertainment venues, cinemas, nightclubs and many restaurants, bars and shops

(🚻 19T ✉ Southbank ☎ 9292 8888 🕐 24 hours daily 🚉 Flinders Street 🚋 Tram 10, 12, 96, 109).

LUXURY HOTELS

Melbourne's accommodation

Melbourne offers every category of accommodation – from backpacker's hostels to international-standard deluxe hotels (A$250-plus per person per night). There are also many economical, self-catering apartments, and reasonably priced guesthouses and hostels are plentiful. Bed-and-breakfasts are numerous, particularly in rural areas close to the city. Melbourne's major hotel areas are the city centre, East Melbourne, North Melbourne and around Southbank.

Prices

Prices are per room per night including tax, regardless of single or double occupancy.

Luxury	A$195–500
Mid-range	A$95–194
Budget	A$55–94

HOTEL COMO
This top hotel offers studios and suites, great food, a gymnasium, sauna and pool. It's near some of Melbourne's most popular shops and restaurants.
🏨 8J ✉ 630 Chapel Street, South Yarra ☎ 9824 0400, fax 9824 1263 🚋 Tram 78, 79

CROWN RESORT
The ultimate in luxury, this hotel, with the casino at its doorstep, has a world-class health centre, classy shopping centres and waterfront restaurants.
🏨 19T ✉ Southbank ☎ 9292 6666, fax 9292 6299 🚉 Flinders Street 🚋 Tram 10, 12, 96, 109

GRAND HYATT MELBOURNE
One of Melbourne's best hotels, the Grand Hyatt has very good restaurants, a health and fitness centre, business facilities and exclusive boutiques.
🏨 21R ✉ 123 Collins Street ☎ 9657 1234, 9650 3491 🚋 City Circle Tram

LE MERIDIEN AT RIALTO
Stylish luxury hotel in a heritage-listed building, with top service, a great location next to the Rialto Towers, bars, and a heated rooftop pool and sauna.
🏨 20S ✉ 495 Collins Street ☎ 9620 911, fax 9614 1219 🚋 City Circle Tram

PARK HYATT MELBOURNE
This luxury hotel provides a warm, distinctive ambience and high levels of service.
🏨 22R ✉ 1 Parliament Place, Melbourne ☎ 9224 1234, fax 9224 1200 🚋 City Circle Tram

SHERATON TOWERS
Close to the Arts Centre action and the Crown Entertainment Complex, this top hotel has a business centre, a health club and a heated pool.
🏨 20T ✉ 1 Brown Street, Southgate, (short walk from city centre) ☎ 9696 3100, fax 9690 5889

HOTEL SOFITEL
One of the city's finest hotels, at the 'Paris end' of Collins Street – so-called for its trees and French-style cafés – only a short walk to Treasury Gardens, in the retail district.
🏨 21R ✉ 25 Collins Street ☎ 9653 0000, fax 9650 4261 🚋 City Circle Tram

STAMFORD PLAZA
This all-suite hotel is within walking distance of theatres, cinemas and the exclusive end of Collins Street.
🏨 21R ✉ 111 Little Collins Street ☎ 9659 1000, fax 9659 0999 🚋 City Circle Tram

WINDSOR HOTEL
One of the world's finest hotels and certainly Australia's grandest and most steeped in history, this Oberoi chain hotel offers fine service and a sense of style. Even if you don't stay here, check it out.
🏨 21R ✉ 103 Spring Street ☎ 9653 0653, fax 9633 6001 🚋 City Circle Tram

MID-RANGE HOTELS

ALL SEASONS WELCOME HOTEL

In a handy location, right in the centre of the city, close to the major department stores and the Central Business District, this popular hotel is very convenient and has great facilities at a reasonable price.

✚ 20R ✉ 265 Little Bourke Street ☎ 9639 0555, fax 9650 3920 🚃 City Circle Tram

BATMAN'S HILL HOTEL

This hotel is just a few minutes stroll from the Crown Entertainment Complex, the Yarra River, the new Colonial Stadium and Spencer Street Station.

✚ 18T ✉ 66 Spencer Street ☎ 9614 6344, fax 9614 1189 🚉 Spencer Street

DOWNTOWNER ON LYGON

Within easy walking distance of the city, the Queen Victoria Market, and the varied restaurants of Lygon Street, this friendly hotel is of a very high standard.

✚ 20P ✉ 166 Lygon Street ☎ 9663 5555, fax 9662 3308 🚃 City Circle Tram

HOTEL GRAND CHANCELLOR

In the heart of the city, with Chinatown and the theatre district on its doorstep, this excellent and comfortable hotel has the feel of many places with much higher rates.

✚ 20Q ✉ 131 Lonsdale Street ☎ 9663 3161, fax 9662 3479 🚃 City Circle Tram

KING BOUTIQUE ACCOMMODATION

This small, attractive hotel has three delightful bedrooms with good facilities and a location that couldn't be bettered, directly opposite the Carlton Gardens. The breakfasts are delicious.

✚ 21N ✉ 122 Nicholson Street, Fitzroy ☎ 9417 1113, fax 9417 1116 🚃 Tram 96

THE PRINCE

Nothing quite matches a stay at this particularly stylish and elegant boutique hotel, home of one of the city's top restaurants, Circa (► 62).

✚ 7L ✉ 2 Acland Street, St Kilda ☎ 9536 1111, fax 9536 1100 🚃 Tram 16

RADISSON ON FLAGSTAFF GARDENS

Conveniently located in the heart of the city, opposite historic Flagstaff Gardens, this 184-room hotel has a health and fitness centre, a business centre, non-smoking floors and valet parking.

✚ 18R ✉ 380 William Street ☎ 9322 8000, fax 9322 8888 🚃 City Circle Tram

ROBINSONS BY THE SEA

Overlooking Port Phillip Bay at St Kilda, this well-known bed-and-breakfast is a classic old Victorian terrace house. The helpful hosts are Wendy and Jonathan.

✚ 7L ✉ 335 Beaconsfield Parade, St Kilda ☎ 9534 2683, fax 9534 2683 🚃 Tram 16

Apartments

Renting quarters in one of Melbourne's apartment-style hotels generally falls into the moderate price range. Many of these apartments, with full maid service, are large enough for families or small groups. They have from one to three bedrooms, with separate dining areas and kitchens or kitchenettes, so you can cook your own meals if it suits you. One of the best of these is Pacific International Suites (✉ 471 Little Bourke Street ☎ 9607 3000), close to the CBD.

Country style

Be sure to experience the green splendour of the Dandenong Ranges, an hour east of the city centre (► 35). One of the best places to stay here is Arcadia Cottages (✉ 188 Falls Road, Olinda ☎ 9751 1017). These superbly furnished and individually crafted cottages are set in an attractive garden and include hot tubs and cosy wood-fired heaters. Be sure to reserve ahead because they are popular.

Budget Hotels & Guesthouses

Backpacker accommodation

Melbourne has many backpacker lodges with accommodation varing from private rooms to dormitories. Prices start at A$10 per night and most places offer reduced rates for long stays. The best backpacker areas are in the city, North Melbourne and the beach suburb of St Kilda.
Another inexpensive accommodation option is staying at the Australian version of the local pub, but often referred to as a hotel. More details can be obtained from the Victorian Tourism Information Service (☎ 132 842).

ASTORIA MOTEL
Not far from the main railway station, this motel is a safe choice, with its own restaurant and good clean rooms.
✚ 18R ✉ 288 Spencer Street
☎ 9670 6801, fax 9670 3034
Ⓢ Spencer Street

CLAREMONT ACCOMMODATION
A conveniently located guesthouse with good communal facilities and bright rooms.
✚ 8J ✉ 189 Toorak Road, South Yarra ☎ 9826 8000, fax 9827 8652 🚋 Tram 8

GEORGIAN COURT GUESTHOUSE
An elegant bed-and-breakfast with a variety of rooms.
✚ 23S ✉ 21 George Street, East Melbourne ☎ 9419 6353, fax 9416 0895 🚋 Tram 48, 75

GLOBAL BACKPACKERS
Just opposite the Queen Victoria Market, this top section of an old pub has good facilities and an indoor rock climbing wall.
✚ 19P ✉ 238 Victoria Street, ☎ 9328 3728, fax 9329 8966 🚋 City Circle Tram

HOTEL Y
A good range of reasonably priced accommodation, plus a fitness and recreation centre, a heated indoor pool and café.
✚ 19Q ✉ 489 Elizabeth Street ☎ 9329 5188, fax 9329 1469 🚋 City Circle Tram

KINGSGATE HOTEL
This renovated private hotel offers rooms with either shared or private bathrooms.
✚ 18S ✉ 131 King Street
☎ 9629 4171, fax 9629 7110
🚋 City Circle Tram

THE NUNNERY
Clean, centrally-heated rooms, comfortable communal facilities, and a great atmosphere ensure that this place remains popular with budget travellers.
✚ 21N ✉ 116 Nicholson Street, Fitzroy ☎ 9419 8637, fax 9417 7736 🚋 Tram 96

QUEENSBURY HILL YHA
Over 300 rooms with fine facilities, a travel agency and good travel information. This is near Queen Victoria Market and not far from the city centre.
✚ 18P ✉ 78 Howard Street, North Melbourne ☎ 9329 8599, fax 9326 8427 🚋 Tram 57

ST KILDA COFFEE PALACE
One of the city's most popular backpackers' hostels, close to the action in St Kilda. Has a rooftop garden, friendly staff and an excellent bulletin board where you can get great travel information.
✚ 7L ✉ 24 Grey Street, St Kilda ☎ 9534 5283, fax 9593 9166 🚋 Tram 16

TOAD HALL
There is a choice of dorm or private rooms at this popular and conveniently located hostel.
✚ 19Q ✉ 441 Elizabeth Street ☎ 9600 9010, fax 9600 9013 🚋 City Circle Tram

MELBOURNE's
travel facts

ARRIVING & DEPARTING

Before you go

- All visitors require a valid passport and an ETA (Electronic Travel Authority). An ETA replaces a visa. It is fully electronic and is available through travel agents.
- A Tourist ETA is valid for one year (or until the expiry date of your passport, if less) and will allow you to stay for a total of three months.
- Vaccination certificates are not normally required, unless you have travelled to an infected country within the previous 14 days.
- Australian Tourist Commission office: ✉ 10 Putney Hill, London SW15 ☎ Administration only: 020 8780 2220. Brochure line: 0870 556 1434

Travel insurance

- Ensure you have appropriate cover before departure.

What to pack

- In summer (December–February) the temperature averages 25°C. Take cotton clothing, a broad-brimmed hat, sunglasses and other summer-weight items, plus an umbrella.
- In winter (June–August) take a raincoat and/or medium-weight coat, plus clothing suitable for an average 13°C.

Climate

- The best time to visit is during the warmer months, generally October–April. Go in winter if you like skiing as facilities are good near Melbourne.
- Melbourne has four distinct seasons free from extremes. It rarely snows and the temperature only rises above 32°C a few times a year.

- Spring (September–November) is cool to mild with average maximums of 20°C and average minimums of 10°C.
- Summer (December–February) is warm to hot with average maximums of 25°C and average minimums of 14°C.
- Autumn (March–May) is mild with average maximums of 20°C and average minimums of 11°C.
- Winter (June–August) is cool to brisk with average maximums of 14°C and average minimums of 7°C.
- Average rainfall – 660mm.

Arriving by air

- Melbourne Airport at Tullamarine is the main port of entry.
- The airport is 22.5km from Melbourne's centre. There are taxis and inexpensive bus services (▶ 91) into the city, as well as car-rental outlets (see below).

Arriving by sea

- Cruise lines that visit Australia include Cunard, P&O and Crystal Cruises.

Travelling from Melbourne

- Numerous daily flights, buses and trains serve all major towns and cities in Australia.

Car hire

- Hiring a car may be necessary for some of the out-of-town trips within this book. You must be over 21. Compulsory third-party insurance is included in rental prices, which are on average A$50–A$70 per day. Overseas visitors require an international driving licence.
- Major Melbourne car rental companies are: Avis ☎ 136 333,

Budget ☎ 132 727 and Hertz
☎ 133 039
- Full details of Australia's road
  rules are available from the
  Australian Automobile
  Association in Canberra ☎ (02)
  6247 7311

Customs regulations

- Visitors aged 18 or over may bring
  in 250 cigarettes or 250g of tobacco
  or cigars; 1,125ml of alcoholic
  spirits; plus other dutiable goods to
  the value of A$400 per person.
- There is no limit on money
  imported for personal use,
  although amounts in excess of
  A$5,000 or its equivalent must be
  declared on arrival.
- The smuggling of all drugs is
  treated harshly in Australia, and
  the importing of firearms and
  items such as ivory or other
  products from endangered
  species is illegal or restricted.

ESSENTIAL FACTS

Electricity

- The electricity supply in Australia
  is 230–250 volts AC. Three-flat-
  pin plugs are the standard but are
  not the same as in the UK and
  adaptors are needed.
- Hotels provide standard 110-volt
  and 240-volt shaver sockets.

Etiquette

- Smoking is prohibited on public
  transport (including all internal
  flights and inside airport
  terminals), in cinemas, theatres,
  shops and shopping centres.
  Many restaurants provide
  non-smoking areas.
- Dress is generally smart-casual.
  Casual clothing for women and
  shorts for men are usual in
  summer, even in the city centre.
- Tipping is expected only in

restaurants. Service charges are
not normally added to bills, so a
10 per cent tip is the norm.
Tipping taxi drivers and hotel
staff is optional.

Goods & Services Tax (GST)

- A 10 percent GST applies to all
  goods and services. The charge is
  sometimes added to bills, but is
  often included in listed prices.

Money matters

- The Australian unit of currency
  is the Australian dollar (A$),
  comprising 100 cents. Banknotes
  come in A$100, A$50, A$20,
  A$10 and A$5 denominations.
  Coins come in 5¢, 10¢, 20¢ and
  50¢ (silver), and A$1 and A$2
  (gold coloured).
- Currency exchanges at hotels
  and other outlets such as
  American Express and Thomas
  Cook are open outside banking
  hours. International airport
  exchange facilities are open daily
  5:30AM–11PM. You can obtain
  cash via your bank or credit card
  at 24-hour automatic teller
  machines (ATMs) that are easily
  found around the city.
- Major credit cards (American
  Express, Visa, MasterCard and
  Bankcard) are widely accepted
  throughout the city.
- Most types and currencies of
  travellers' cheques can be cashed
  at the airport, banks, larger
  hotels, tourist centres and shops.

National, state and school holidays

- 1 January: New Year's Day
  26 January: Australia Day
  2nd Monday in March: Labour
  Day (Victorian state holiday)
  Good Friday
  Easter Monday
  25 April: Anzac Day

2nd Monday in June: Queen's Birthday
1st Tuesday in November: Melbourne Cup
25 December: Christmas Day
26 December: Christmas holiday
- School summer holidays are mid-December to late January – transport, accommodation and tourist facilities are heavily booked at this time.

Opening hours
- Shops: in the city centre generally open Mon–Thu 10–6; Fri 10–9; Sat and Sun 10–6. Suburban hours vary; corner shops often open daily 8–8 or later.
- Banks: Mon–Thu 9:30–4; Fri 9:30–5. City head-office banks open Mon–Fri 8:15–5.
- Hotels (pubs): generally 10AM–11PM.
- Museums and galleries: generally daily 10–5. Some close on one day of the week and hours may vary from day to day.
- Offices: Mon–Fri 9–5 (5:30 in some cases).
- Restaurants: some close on Sun or Mon.

Places of worship
- Anglican: St Paul's Cathedral ✉ Corner of Swanston and Flinders streets
- Roman Catholic: St Patrick's Cathedral ✉ Cathedral Place
- Baptist ✉ 174 Collins Street
- Orthodox Jewish: East Melbourne Synagogue ✉ 488 Albert Street, East Melbourne ☎ 9962 1372
- Buddhist: Buddhist Centre ☎ 9380 4303
- Muslim: City Mosque ✉ 66 Jeffcott Street, West Melbourne ☎ 9328 2067

Student travellers
- International Student Identity Cards are not usually recognised by cinemas, theatres or public transport authorities, but you may be able to get concessions on bus travel.
- There are many backpackers' lodges, YHA establishments and hostels in Melbourne (all busy in summer). YHA cardholders *may* obtain discounts.

Time differences
- Australia has three major time zones, with Melbourne and other eastern cities on Eastern Standard Time (EST), 10 hours ahead of GMT.
- Between late October and March most states adopt Summer Time (daylight saving) – Melbourne is then 11 hours ahead of GMT.
- Based on standard time, Melbourne is 15 hours ahead of New York and 18 hours ahead of San Francisco.

Toilets
- Free public toilets are found in parks, public places, galleries, museums, department stores and also in bus and railway stations. Most hotels will allow you to use their facilities.

Tourist information
- Victorian Tourism Information Service ☎ 132 842
- City of Melbourne ☎ 9658 9658 🕐 Mon–Fri 9–5 covers a range of accommodation.
- City Experience Centre ✉ Corner of Collins and Swanston streets ☎ 9658 9955 features interactive tourist information about sightseeing.

Women travellers
- Melbourne is generally a safe place for women travellers. Walking alone in parks or on beaches at night, and travelling alone on out-of-city-centre trains at night is not recommended.

PUBLIC TRANSPORT

- For all timetable and ticket enquiries (buses, ferries and Cityrail trains), call ☎ 131 638 (daily 7AM–9PM) and for VicRail (out of town) train details call ☎ 9563 4744

Buses

- Melbourne's buses vary in colour, depending on company.
- The Airport Express runs between Melbourne Airport and the city terminus.
- Privately run Explorer buses take passengers around the sights.
- There are no specific bus terminals for suburban buses. Catch them at designated stops.
- Ordinary tickets are available on board. Buy special passes (see below) at kiosks and news-agencies as well as from the driver.
- Privately run Nightrider Buses can take you home safely between 12:30AM and 4:30AM on Saturday or Sunday mornings for A$5. They head for various suburban destinations and run at hourly intervals, picking up at designated stops, including those close to major nightlife venues.
- Skybus runs to Melbourne Airport, around the clock, daily. Drop-offs and pick-ups are available at hotels and at Spencer Street Station. Cost is A$10 for adults and A$4.50 for children ☎ 9335 3066

Ferries

- Ferries run from Southgate and from Princes Bridge wharves. These are primarily for tours but a ferry runs to Williamstown as public transport.
- Buy tickets directly from the operators.

Taxis

- Taxis are meter-operated, yellow, and conspicuously marked with a 'Taxi' sign on top of the vehicle. The basic charge is around A$2.80 and the remainder of the fare is calculated based on time and distance (A$1.15 per kilometre). A small additional booking fee is charged for taxis ordered by phone. A surcharge of A$1.10 applies after midnight.
- Taxis are abundant.
- Main operators include Arrow ☎ 132 211; Black Cabs ☎ 132 227; Embassy ☎ 131 755; and Silver Top ☎ 131 008. Ask for a taxi that can take a wheelchair if you need one.

Tickets, maps, and discounts

- Metcard tickets allow for travel on trams, trains and buses within the zones marked on the ticket. Three fare zones apply: Zone 1 covers most of the CBD area and inner suburbs. Zones 2 and 3 extend to the outer fringes of the Melbourne area.
- A two-hour ticket (A$2.30 and up) allows unlimited travel for two hours, daily tickets (A$4.40 and up) for the whole day. Short-trip tickets, two-hour tickets and 60 Plus tickets for senior citizens may be purchased on board trams and buses. All Metcard tickets can be bought at railroad stations from Customer Service Centres and vending machines, at retail outlets displaying the Metcard sign or flag, and at the City Met Shop at 103 Elizabeth Street.
- Free public transport maps are available at stations and the Met Shop in Elizabeth Street.

Trains

- Melbourne's inner-city rail lines include the City Loop

(Parliament, Melbourne Central, Flagstaff Gardens, Spencer Street and Flinders Street Station).
- Flinders Street Station is the main suburban rail terminus.
- Buy tickets from booths or machines, and enter platforms via the automatic barriers.
- Trains operate 5AM–midnight Mon–Sat, 8AM–11PM Sun.

Trams
- Service is extensive and frequent, and this is the best way to travel.
- Principal services operate from Swanston and Elizabeth streets (north and south); Flinders, Collins and Bourke streets and Batman Avenue (east and west). Trams operate between 5AM and midnight Mon–Sat, and 8AM and 11PM Sun.
- The free City Circle Tram runs in both directions around the entire city centre, at 10-minute intervals, between 10AM and 6PM daily.

MEDIA & COMMUNICATIONS

International newsagents
- UK and US newspapers, as well as many foreign-language papers, are available from larger newsagents around the city centre, including Mitty's News Agency, 53 Bourke Street.

Magazines
- The weekly *Bulletin* is Australia's answer to *Time* and *Newsweek*.

Newspapers
- The main national daily newspaper is *The Australian*; read *The Australian Financial Review* for business news.

- The city's daily newspapers are the *The Age*, giving a reasonable coverage of international news and *The Herald Sun*, a tabloid-style paper published in several editions throughout the day.

Post offices and postage
- Post offices are generally open Mon–Fri 9–5. Melbourne General Post Office hours are Mon–Fri 8:15–5:30; Sat 8:30–noon.
- Larger post offices sell airmails, and provide fax and e-mail facilities.
- Stamps can also be purchased in hotels and from some newsagents and souvenir shops.

Radio
- Melbourne has 13 major stations, ranging from FM rock music broadcasters such as Triple J-FM and Triple M-FM to the Australian Broadcasting Corporation's (ABC) Radio National and 3LO. There are also many AM music, chat and news stations.

Telephones
- Public telephones are found at phone booths, post offices, hotels, petrol stations, shops, railway and bus stations, and cafés.
- Local calls cost 40¢ for unlimited time.
- Long-distance calls within Australia, known as STD calls, vary considerably in price, but you should have a good supply of A50¢ and A$1 coins. Calls are cheaper after 6PM and on weekends.
- ☎ 012 (0176 from pay phones) for operator assistance.
- ☎ 011 for bookings and reverse-charge calls.
- Phonecards come in values of

A$2 to A$20; credit cards can also be used from some phones.

- International calls, known as ISD calls, can be made from your hotel and certain public telephones by dialing ☎ 0011, followed by the country codes: UK 44; USA and Canada 1; France 33; Germany 49. For international enquiries ☎ 0102. To book an operator-connected call ☎ 0101
- To call a Melbourne or Victoria number from outside the state, use the prefix 03. Calls from within the state require no prefix.

Television

- ABC (Australian Broadcasting Corporation) Channel 2 has no commercials.
- Melbourne has four commercial stations: Channels 7, 9, 10 and SBS (Special Broadcasting Service).
- Cable services are available in most major hotels.

EMERGENCIES

Emergency phone numbers

- Police, ambulance or fire: ☎ 000 (24 hours). Calls are free.

Consulates

- Canada: ☎ 9811 9999
- France: ☎ 9820 0921
- Germany: ☎ 9864 6888
- UK: ☎ 9650 4155
- USA: ☎ 9526 5900

Medical treatment

- Doctors and dentists are readily available and there are many medical centres where appointments are not necessary.
- Hotels will help you locate a doctor.
- Medical, dental and ambulance

services are excellent, but costly.
- British, New Zealand, and some other nationals are entitled to 'immediate necessary treatment' under a reciprocal agreement. Dental services are not included.

Medicines

- Visitors are permitted to bring prescribed medications in reasonable amounts. Bring your prescription and leave medications in their original containers to avoid problems at customs. Most prescription drugs are widely available.

Police

- The non-emergency police number is ☎ 9247 6666
- Melbourne's police wear blue uniforms and a peaked cap. They are generally helpful and polite.

Sensible precautions

- If you experience a theft or any other incident, report it to your hotel and to the police. If your travellers' cheques are stolen, advise the relevant organisation.
- It is safe to drink tap water.
- The only medical problems you are likely to experience are sunburn and mosquito bites.
- For sun protection, make sure you have good supplies of SPF 15+ block, and wear sunglasses, a hat and long sleeves if you burn easily; avoid the summer sun in the middle of the day.
- Dangerous currents and marine stingers can cause problems in the sea in summer. Swim only at beaches with lifeguards and observe any posted warnings.
- If you undertake long hikes, let someone know of your expected return time.

INDEX

CityPack
Melbourne

Written by   Rod Ritchie
Edited, designed and produced by
     AA Publishing
Maps   © Periplus Editions 2001

ISBN 0 7495 2921 0

Published by AA Publishing (a trading name of Automobile Association Developments Limited, whose registered office is Millstream, Maidenhead Road, Windsor, Berkshire SL4 5GD. Registered number 1878835).

Colour separation by Daylight Colour Art Pte Ltd, Singapore
Printed and bound by Dai Nippon Printing Co (Hong Kong) Ltd.

Acknowledgements

The Automobile Association would like to thank the following photographers, libraries and agencies for their assistance in the preparation of this book:
Auscape 13b, 26a, 33, 57b, 58, 87b (Jean-Paul Ferrero); 41b (Guy Lamothe); 1, 7, 13a, 15, 16, 18, 20, 23a, 23b, 24, 25b, 26b, 27, 29b, 32a, 32b, 34b, 36a, 38a, 38b, 39a, 39b, 41a, 41b, 43a, 45, 46a, 46b, 47a, 47b, 48a, 48b, 59, 60, 61a, 87a (Jean-Marc La Roque); 6, 29a, 54 (Mike Leonard); 50 (D Parer & E Parer-Cook); Australian Tourist Commission 21; Getty One/Stone front cover, main; Lone Pines Sanctuary 5a; Mary Evans Picture Library 8; Melbourne Aquarium 40a, 40b; Melbourne Gaol 30a, 30b; Melbourne Immigration Museum 42a, 42b; Melbourne Museum of Modern Art 44a, 44b; Melbourne Museum 25a; Melbourne Scienceworks 57a; Montsalvat 53; Powerstock/Zefa cover a, b; Rialto Towers 34a; R Sloane 17, 52; Spectrum Colour Library 31; Tourism Victoria 19, 28, 35, 36b, 37, 55, 56. The rest of the images are held in the Assoication's own Library (AA Photo Library) and were taken by Adrian Baker 49, Paul Kenward 61b, Christine Osbourne 5b.

MANAGING EDITOR *Hilary Weston*
COPY EDITOR *Julia Walkden*

A01582

Titles in the Citypack series
● Amsterdam ● Bangkok ● Barcelona ● Beijing ● Berlin ● Boston ●
● Brussels & Bruges ● Chicago ● Dublin ● Florence ● Hong Kong ● Lisbon ●
London ● Los Angeles ● ● Madrid ● Melbourne ● Miami ● Montréal ● Munich ●
New York ● Paris ● Prague ● Rome ● San Francisco ● Seattle ● Shanghai ●
● Singapore ● Sydney ● Tokyo ● Toronto ● Venice ● Vienna ● Washington ●